What people are saying ab

My Be

I appreciate the transparency of Pam's writing. The way she approaches God is refreshing. Pam's honesty about being afraid to step out of her comfort zone allows the reader to be okay with their own insecurities. I felt as if God was personally speaking to me.

—Kim Chaffin, author of *Simply Blessed*

I am excited for you to read Pam Bacani's new book, *My Beloved.* She has great insight into the healing power of the Holy Spirit for both our physical and spiritual bodies, and her stories illustrate it. Pam and her family are faithful in serving at Living Stone Church. Every week, Pam brings a shepherd's heart to broken and hurting people.

—Pastor Van Bradeen, Lead Pastor at Living Stone Church of Spokane, author of *Live Love: Becoming Like Christ in Thought, Speech, and Action*

Clearly Pam's heart bursts with profound love for God. Her inspirational messages are sweet, crisp, and purely written. Most admirably, Pam is persistent in giving glory to whom it belongs. Her unique style evokes the beloved reader to press on and remain fixed on His promises.

—Jannis Hibberts, author of *Tricky Ricky* The Homestead Twins series

Pam Bacani is anointed to release the atmosphere of Heaven. *My Beloved's* scope is multi-generational. Pam's encouragement to "make memories with the Spirit today" is an invitation for every believer to join this holy expedition with the potential to change our natural perspective. Each page contains wisdom to be applied and wielded over your family and circle of influence.

—Jessica Gerdes, Fellow Student of the Spirit

My Beloved is written for those who desire to go to deeper places with God and to develop a relationship of intimacy. Pam Bacani shares her own journey to the Father's heart. She lives the truth of Song of Solomon 6:3, *I am my beloved's and my beloved is mine.* The daily readings will challenge you to abide in Christ and to live in His love. Learn from Pam the simple, yet powerful ways of walking with the Holy Spirit. You will be activated to touch those around you with fresh hope and joy along with a greater awareness of God's goodness and grace.

—Sharon Murphy, Director of Transformation Prayer, Healing Rooms, author of *Transforming Our Land and Cities*

Jeane -
When I anointed your book I felt the Lord say your hearts cry is that you would walk holy + blameless before the Lord all the days of your life. That you would have clean hands and a pure heart and stand on God's holy mountain with Him! He has heard your prayers for purity and answered them.

Blessed are the pure in heart, for they will see God -
Matthew 5:8

That is your scripture my dear! ♡

Jeane -
God has purified you with Hyssop. It was the hyssop branch that went up to Jesus mouth as He was dying on a tree, when He declared, "It is Finished!" You have been Clothed in White robes. Robes of righteousness are yours because of Christ. You are radiant and beautiful to Him!

My Beloved

(Jesus paid it all by Kristian Stanfill Song for you ♡)

A Journey into the Arms of Abba Father

I pray He blesses you abundantly this next year & that you see yourself & others through His eyes and declare that truth regardless of what you are seeing in the natural.

Pam Bacani

Remember Always, He calls you saint now, not sinner!!
Praise Jesus
Blessings & ♡ Pam Bacani

Published by Isaiah Sixty 1:1 With Him Ministries
Deer Park, Washington

Softcover ISBN: 978-1-7339174-0-7
ebook ISBN: 978-1-7339174-1-4

Graphic design by: Christine Dupre
Edited by: Barbara Hollace
Book design by: Russel Davis, Gray Dog Press

To contact the author for more information or to share your testimonies,
email: pbacanimybeloved@gmail.com

Printed in the United States of America

Acknowledgments

I want to thank God for equipping me to fulfill my calling to be a writer. His ways are far beyond anything I could have imagined. The Holy Spirit was my constant guide and reminded me of the truth of who I was and what God called me to do. God's grace was my constant companion. With God's help, I did something I never thought I could do. God didn't look at the special ed classes or the fact that I barely passed high school. I praise my heavenly Father for overlooking my lack of ability and my insecurity, and empowering me to trust Him. The Bible says, "All things are possible to those who believe." I believed. Glory to God!

To my wonderful family, thank you for being flexible and willing to let me pursue this dream. You gave me grace and helped with the chores so I could write. Thank you for helping me to fulfill His calling. I love you all so much.

Thank you, Toni Burke, for believing that my writing could help others. You were the first to open the door to writing as I wrote blog posts for your ministry. Writing that first blog was difficult but your encouragement helped me to continue writing.

Jannis Bacani, Van Bradeen, and Kim Chaffin, thank you for being forerunners as authors yourselves. Your encouragement and advice were greatly needed and appreciated.

To Jessica Gerdes and Sharon Murphy, thank you for continually calling me to think higher, like Christ. Your encouragement to pursue God and the things above drove me into His arms on a regular basis.

To all those prophetic people who prophesied that I would write a book, Thank you! Seeds of faith were planted through the words you spoke and today we reap the first harvest through this book, *My Beloved.*

Most of all, I want to thank Barb Hollace, my editor, friend, and sister in Christ. This book could not have been completed without her writing expertise or her relationship with God. Her wisdom was invaluable. Barb's dedication and integrity to bringing God glory through this book was astounding. Her prayers coupled with mine, infused by the will of the Father, is why you are holding this book in your hands.

Foreword

Oil and perfume make the heart glad,
So a man's counsel is sweet to his friend
Proverbs 27:9

God placed this book in Pam's heart long before her calling to be a writer surfaced. Just like this book, GOD brings people into your life when you least expect it. One winter morning as my family and I walked into Living Stone Church in Spokane, Washington, we met a beautiful, petite blonde woman with the most welcoming smile standing at the rear of the church. Pam's smile was contagious, her passion for Christ burst forth like a ray of sunshine after the rain. During the service as I watched Pam praise and worship the Lord, all I could ask myself was, "How do I find THAT in my life?"

During this time, GOD was doing a tremendous work in my life. I was desperately searching and praying for a friend but I needed someone who understood what GOD meant to me and also desired to seek His face daily. That special friend I could share my innermost thoughts with, but most of all, would pray with me. On a beautiful spring morning, GOD answered my prayer when I took that first brave step across the church and asked Pam if she would be interested in writing a blog post for my blog, *A Woman's Heart*. It takes courage to step out of your comfort zone, even when the gift is from God's heart to yours.

Since the day of our first encounter, I have learned so much from Pam. Her love and passion for God and her family have rekindled the fire in me, personally. Pam's posts are GOD-inspired with wisdom, truth, and love including how to listen to GOD's heart, pray with intensity, and remember, we are vessels for Him.

This book was written through many hours of prayer and because of GOD's love for you. If you close your eyes, you will meet GOD face-to-face through Pam's writing. Jesus became flesh to make GOD's spiritual blessings known to the world. Today, He is alive and uses people for this same purpose. Pam is that vessel, a vessel of honor for GOD capturing and outlining His desires for us through scripture and prayer. Walking by faith, Pam stands firm in His love. But most of all, her heart's desire is for you to walk in freedom knowing Him, freedom to know who you are in Christ.

Blessings to all,
Toni Burke
A Woman's Heart

Contents

Holy In His Sight

Communing with God

Embracing Jesus, our First Love

Live By the Spirit

The Victorious Life

Ambassadors for Christ

Introduction

My Beloved

A Journey into the Arms of Abba Father

The next 55 days will change your life. God's love and everlasting grace are woven through the pages of this book, *My Beloved.* As you hear His voice and listen to His heart beat for you, be open to hearing His truth. You may be asking, "Why 55 days?" The number "50" refers to Pentecost. From the time of Jesus' death until the time the disciples received the baptism in the Holy Spirit was 50 days. You, too, shall be thoroughly drenched in the Holy Spirit while reading this book. Additionally, the number five belongs to the virtue of grace from our Everlasting Father. May a double portion of His grace rest upon you.

My Beloved is a work of prophetic encouragement through my life's journey of trusting God. Finding my way up onto His lap and resting in His arms has been one of the hardest, yet most valuable lessons I've ever learned. God has gently led me from my old mindset to a new path of righteous living and pursuing His heart. Transformation is an ongoing condition for the believer who is submitted to Christ. It is a process that will encompass all the days of our lives. *My Beloved* will exhort you to live a life pleasing to God and Him alone. You will be encouraged to see yourself through His eyes of love rather than man's eyes, and then challenged to see others in the same light. *My Beloved* will urge you to think higher, step into your destiny, and live a life of action and love. Come and join me as we pursue His highest and best!

How to Use This Book

The 55 days in this devotional are divided into eight themes. There are seven sections for each day:

1. **Scripture verse:** Memorize the scripture and speak it out loud. Transform the way you think by declaring God's words.

2. **Thought for the Day:** Connected to the day's theme, take a moment to meditate on it.

3. **Author's Reflection:** Through the author's experience, thoughts, and reflections, you will see God at work and His desire to be part of your everyday life too.

4. **The Lord's Heart:** Read this section as if the Lord is speaking to you personally.

5. **Declaration:** Declare God's truth over you. Declarations have the ability to transform your negative thinking into holy, heavenly thinking.

6. **Prayer:** When you pray, God moves. He bends down and listens to the cries of your heart.

7. **His Heart for Me:** Listen to what God is saying related to the questions/suggestions in this section. Write down whatever He reveals to you and then take action.

My Prayer for You

Abba Father, wrap Your loving arms around each person who reads this book and let them feel and experience Your powerful presence each day. Pour out Your love in abundant ways, ways that leave them breathless and in awe of You. Put a desire in their heart to climb up on Your lap and rest, as they learn to hear Your heart beat for them. May they know the hope of their calling and empower them to walk in complete obedience to You.

Holy Spirit, I ask that You become more active and known in each reader's life, unleashing and activating the gifts and fruits within them. Continually baptize them in power, love, and truth. May their internal rivers of living water never run dry. Always give them eyes to see the Lord's goodness and faithfulness, despite their earthly circumstances.

As you read *My Beloved,* may your love for Christ be stirred up to a level of full intimate adoration awaiting His return. May the spirit of joy and fun be upon you. Receive a new level of freedom in your life, for wherever the Spirit of the Lord is, there is freedom. May you walk in the power of His Spirit and in the love of Christ continually. As you receive increased heart knowledge of who He is, may you love Him even more. Let greater knowledge of who you are, that causes you to walk in His resurrection power from on high, be your portion. May He open the heavens over you and teach you about His Kingdom, and all that is available to you as a beloved saint. May a new level of intimacy be yours.

In Christ our Lord. Amen.

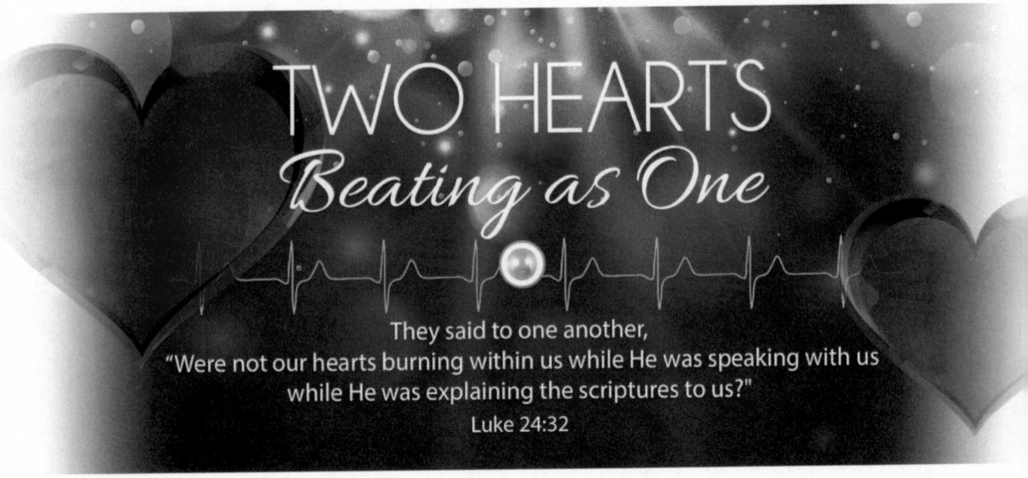
TWO HEARTS
Beating as One
They said to one another,
"Were not our hearts burning within us while He was speaking with us
while He was explaining the scriptures to us?"
Luke 24:32

Day 1

A Place of Solitude

He who dwells in the shelter of the Most High
Will abide in the shadow of the Almighty.
Psalm 91:1

Thought for the Day: The secret place is not only a physical place but a state of your soul; an awareness of His presence.

My habit of slipping away to be with Jesus often leaves my family wondering where I am. Now they just assume I am in the forest praying. Some may call it, selfish. I call it wisdom, knowing when I need a timeout.

A secret place is a place where I won't be interrupted by family, phone calls, or animals wanting attention. My favorite secret spots include my closet, our small forest, or sitting in my car. When I wake up an hour earlier than everyone else, I can have that quiet time with the Lord I desperately need. Throughout my day, I retreat to the secret place in my soul. It is a place of peace and rest.

Jesus often slipped away to the mountains to be with God. He stayed up late talking with God and sometimes His prayers extended into the morning hours. Jesus knew the importance of spending one-on-one time with His heavenly Father without any interruptions, even when people wanted to be with Him. Matthew 14:23 says that Jesus dismissed the crowds and went up the mountain to pray in solitude. We, too, should seek to spend time with God in our own secret place. When I make time to spend with Jesus, I never walk away disappointed. I always walk away refreshed and renewed.

However, we cannot forget our other responsibilities. Learn to have an awareness of His presence wherever you are, wherever you go.

The Lord's Heart

Dear child, I want you to constantly live in the secret place with Me. Do you know that you can be busy at work and still be with Me in the secret place? In our secret place, you don't doubt Me. In our secret place, you have peace knowing that the great I AM is with you all day long. When you surrender to My Spirit and My will, you live in the secret place. I like it when you take time to get away with Me, just the two of us. This time is precious to Me and I bless you every time you do this. You can live in the secret place of My presence all day long. Invite Me into your day, and look for Me.

When you spend one-on-one time with Me, you get to know Me more. I know everything about you, but you don't know everything about Me. I long for you to know Me. When you meet with Me, come with an expectation that I will meet you there and move in your midst. As I meet with you, I will transform you and give you My thoughts. I will refresh your soul in the quiet place. To live in My presence all day long, you must have a conscious awareness that I am there with you and in you.

For in the day of trouble He will conceal me in His tabernacle;
In the secret place of His tent He will hide me;
He will lift me up on a rock.
Psalm 27:5

Declaration

He will meet me in the secret place of my heart.

Prayer

Abba Father, I long to spend time with You just like Jesus did. Help me to find time in my busy schedule to sit with You in my own secret place. Aid me to live in constant awareness of Your presence throughout my days. I declare this awareness will transform my day and my relationships. It will transform the very depths of my soul. Thank you for concealing me in Your tent of protection. Holy Spirit, I will allow You into all the places of my heart thus causing me to walk in newness of life, spirit, and truth.

In Christ our Lord. Amen.

His Heart for Me

Do you have a secret place where you can be with Jesus and not get interrupted? Find one that works for you. Are you aware of God's presence throughout your day? If not, what can you do to slow down to sense Him? My husband used to set a one-hour timer as a reminder to think about Jesus and pray. This worked for him. Find time to be with Jesus but don't get religious about it. Enjoy your time in His Presence.

Day 2

Praising Our Maker

Sing to the Lord a new song; Sing to the Lord, all the earth.
Sing to the Lord, bless His name; Proclaim good tidings of
His salvation from day to day.
Tell of His glory among the nations, His wonderful deeds among all the
peoples. For great is the Lord and greatly to be praised.
Psalm 96:1-4

Thought for the Day: From the depths of my soul, I will praise You with all that I am.

Our praise displaces the enemy in our lives and changes the atmosphere. Praise changes our negative mindset by renewing our mind and opening the heavens over us. The Lord loves to be praised and worshiped. Praise the Lord in silence, without music playing. Use your mouth to make your own joyful noise. Praise Him freely. Let your whole body worship Him. He adores our heartfelt praise.

One morning this praise sprang forth from my mouth:

> *Lord, I just want to thank you for giving me your Holy Spirit. I don't ever want to do life without Your presence. The day I received the baptism in the Holy Spirit and spoke in tongues was the greatest miracle in my life after my salvation. Thank you, Lord! I never thought it was possible to have a relationship with You like this. I never knew I could know Your thoughts towards me, actually know them deep within my spirit, not just head knowledge, but heart knowledge. Now I know Your great love for me. Your Spirit enables me to speak about Christ everywhere I go. This shy person now has the strength to speak out. I am amazed at what You have planned*

for my life. Thank you for revealing some of Your plans to me. You don't withhold Your heart from us, You share Your secrets.

Today is a day to praise You for all You do in our lives. Thank you for choosing to work through the weak and broken to reach the lost and perishing around us. Praise and glory to You, God Almighty. Thank you for the joy that comes from living and walking like Jesus walked. What a privilege it is to continue the work of Christ. Thank you for the power of Your Spirit within us to raise the dead, cast out demons, and heal the sick. We rejoice in the fact that our names are written in heaven. Holy, Holy, Holy are You, God. Your plans are marvelous and great for Your beloved children. Hallelujah. Amen.

The Lord's Heart

Oh, how I love it when you praise Me. Let your praises flow towards Me, beloved, for I am your beloved. When you turn to praise Me, I make you more humble, precious one, for your eyes are no longer on yourself but Me. Come into My courts and give a shout to Me. Praise Me according to the mercy, grace, and love I have poured out on you. Praise Me for the gift of salvation through the death of My Son. Praise Me for My glorious plans for your life. Make music to Me, My child. Praise Me in spirit and truth, unhindered and unashamed. Don't worry about what others might think or say about your worship, it is not for them but for Me, and I love it no matter what it looks like or sounds like. Be free to worship Me as you desire. I am worthy of your affections and praise; the great I AM is worthy of it all. Do you want to make Me smile? Your obedience to My Word and unhindered praises make Me smile. Let everything that is within you bless My holy name. Boast in Me, beloved.

Through Him then, let us continually offer up a sacrifice of praise to God, that is, the fruit of lips that give thanks to His name.
Hebrews 13:15

Declaration

He is worthy of all my praise.

Prayer

Abba Father, bring awareness to my mind to praise Your holy name with all that is within me. Holy Spirit, enable me to worship and praise God unhindered by fear of what others might think. I shall remember that I am dancing, singing, and worshipping for an audience of one—You, my Lord, the maker of heaven and earth. I declare that I will praise you in the storm as well as when things are going great. I will worship You in spirit and truth all the days of my life. Praise and worship are how I fight my battles. Continually, I shall set my mind on the things above.

In Christ our Lord. Amen.

His Heart for Me

Write out your praises for the Lord here. If a song or word is bubbling up, let it out. If you want to clap and jump around, do that. Go for it! God is watching and is smiling upon your praises. When David leaped and danced before the Lord in front of others, they probably thought he was young, immature, and maybe even crazy. King David didn't care what others thought and neither should we.

Day 3

His Unconditional Love

If you then, being evil, know how to give good gifts to your children, how much more will your Father who is in heaven give what is good to those who ask Him!
Matthew 7:11

Thought for the Day: God is our perfect Father.

Our relationship with our earthly father shapes our vision of our heavenly Father. Some of us were blessed with good fathers and others only know pain and hurt. If we grew up with a distant earthly father, we will believe our heavenly Father is distant. If we grew up with a father who spent time with us and loved on us, then our view of Abba will be the same.

Growing up without the same consistent father affected my ability to understand my heavenly Father. My birth dad died from cancer when I was two and a half. As a result, my mom moved us closer to her family and remarried when I was four to a good, kind man who loved me to the best of his ability, based on how he was loved as a child. I often felt disconnected from my stepdad who was a busy man, working both outside the home and keeping up the farm where we lived.

My second stepfather was the opposite. We had a blast together including having ice cream after school and going to baseball games. He quickly became my best friend until I realized he was grooming me for his evil intentions to have sexual relations with him. At first when I said no, it was no big deal. But as I continued to say no, his anger rose, and he started physically lashing out at me. The love I thought was real was a lie. I was completely devastated by this deception.

As a result of my experience, my perception of God was very distorted. It kept me away from Him for many years because I believed that God had better things to do than to care about me. I assumed God to be distant and unloving. As I got older, new misconceptions were added. Because I wasn't perfect, I believed that God was angry with me. I didn't trust Him or His plans for me. To be honest, I thought He just wanted to lay down a bunch of rules for me to obey without connection, communication, or love. I didn't want any part of that.

Oh, how wrong I was! By the grace and mercy of God, He drew me in. The scriptures brought me to an awareness of how wonderful and flawless the love of our heavenly Father is. May you know this truth, too.

With His patient enduring love, I now know my "Daddy" for who He truly is. He loves us unconditionally. God longs to spend time with us just because He loves us. Our heavenly Father wants to talk with us and listens to us daily. He is your perfect "Father," lacking nothing. No matter what your relationship with your earthly father has been like, know beyond any doubt that your heavenly Father loves you unconditionally.

The Lord's Heart

I am a good Father to you. I listen intently. Your every need, every question, and every concern is important. I am not distracted when you talk to Me, I don't tune you out. My Spirit leans in to listen to you and your requests. My gifts to you are always good. There is no need to fear Me. I am not like your earthly father. My love is not dependent on what you do or say. I don't withdraw My love from you when you sin or make a mistake. Never will I turn My back on you or throw up My righteous hands and say, "I'm done trying with this one." No, I don't have thoughts like that.

Before you loved Me, I loved you. When I chose the cross for My Son, I had you in mind. Yes, it is true! I loved you so much that I allowed My Son to die for you, before you even knew Me. This is radical love. I accept you just the way you are. You don't need to try to be better, just love Me back. Over time My Spirit will lead you to live righteously. I don't expect you to be perfect so stop requiring that of yourself. My plans and ways are perfect. Follow Me and be willing to let go of anything that I reveal is not pleasing to Me. I am never too busy to listen to your questions or requests. Seek Me, My timing, and My revelation for your life.

And He was saying, "Abba! Father! All things are possible for You; remove this cup from Me; yet not what I will, but what You will."
Mark 14:36

Declaration

God is my Abba Father, perfect in every way.

Prayer

Abba Father, I am so grateful for Your perfect and unconditional love. Expose every lie I am believing about You as my Father and reveal Your truth. The truth of who You are will prevail in my life! I renounce the thought that You are unloving and distant. Bring the truth of who You are to those who are fatherless, to those who have fathers in jail, to those who had fathers with evil intentions. Reveal what a good Father is like, Lord, to us all. May those who know You as a good Father share that knowledge with others. In Christ our Lord. Amen.

His Heart for Me

How is your relationship with your earthly dad? Do you assume God is like your earthly dad in any way? Are your perceptions of God accurate or are they distorted? I encourage you to search the scriptures and find out just how awesome and perfect our heavenly Father is. Here are a few scriptures to get you started. Deuteronomy 32:10, Isaiah 64:8, Psalm 68:5-6, Matthew 6:8, Matthew 6:26, Matthew 18:14, Luke 15:20-24, 2 Corinthians 6:18 and Ephesians 3:20-21.

Day 4

I Am Worthy

I have loved you with an everlasting love;
Therefore I have drawn you with lovingkindness.
Jeremiah 31:3

Thought for the Day: I am loved beyond measure by the Father and Jesus.

PAM: I don't feel worthy of your love, Lord. I have made so many mistakes and committed so many sins. I feel guilty and full of shame. Are you sure You want to love me? Don't I disgust You?

JESUS: (With a tear running down His cheek) No, you don't disgust Me! Drop that stinky trash bag of sins you keep dragging around. You keep placing your sins before Me, and I've already tossed them away, never to be found again. There will be an accounting of your life. But don't you know that My blood saturates the pages. My blood erased your sins. Your faith-filled, spirit-led works are before the Father now, that is what He sees.

Every time you obey Me and follow My leading for your life, gold and glitter lands on those pages of your life in heaven. Don't stand far away from Me thinking you can't come to Me. The enemy wants you to keep that trash bag full of past and present sins, and stand far away. That guilt and shame is not from Me. Throw it away, today! The restraints that held that weight were broken at Golgotha. Step into the freedom I won for you at the cross. Don't make My death null and void by thinking My blood doesn't cover <u>all</u> your sins. It is finished! Remember? Repent and move on, child. Believe you are forgiven and stand firm in the victory won for you. Again, I say to you:

IT IS FINISHED AND COVERED IN MY BLOOD!

You have been set free to love and serve Me, and Me alone.

The Lord's Heart

I loved you before I formed you, dear child. My creative touch, compassion, and love went into forming the very person you are. The details of your life were written in My book before you were born. You are precious in My eyes and honored by Me because I love you. I gave up My Son for you. I reached down and saved you because of My lovingkindness, not anything you could have ever done for Me. My mercy, love, and compassion are what moved My hand to rescue you. I have made you a royal priest in My Kingdom through grace and faith, isn't that fantastic? I will continue to pour out grace upon you, more grace upon more grace throughout all your life.

Everything you think disgusts Me is covered under the blood of Christ. My forgiveness is a free gift given to you. Reach out and grab your free gift today, no strings or hidden agenda is attached to My free gift of grace, just love Me back. My love for you is perfect, not lacking in any way. My love is so abundant and overwhelmingly good that it will quiet your soul. Your shackles and chains have been broken off you and thrown into the sea. Don't go diving for them. My radical and abundant love for you is so great, My child, that I was willing to send My Son to the cross to die for your sins. It was the only way that we could be reconciled and enjoy the intimate relationship I desire to have with all of My children. Because of My Son's sacrifice, now you can be brought into My Kingdom and spend eternity with Us. You are worthy of all My Son's pain. Let that soak in today, beloved. You are loved with an everlasting love.

Knowing that you were not redeemed with perishable things like silver or gold from your futile way of life inherited from your forefathers, but with precious blood, as of a lamb unblemished and spotless, the blood of Jesus Christ.

1 Peter 1:18-19

Declaration

I was worth saving.

Prayer

Abba Father, thank you for shedding Your Son's blood for my redemption, because I was worth saving in Your eyes. Thank you for drawing me into Your Kingdom and for wanting to spend eternity with me. Your love is completely satisfying to my soul. Let Your grace continually be upon me. Holy Spirit, renew my mind as I take in the truth that I am a royal priest in God's Kingdom. Predestined for spirit-led good works He has written on my scroll in heaven. May I be the best ambassador of Christ that I can be while here on earth, not in my own strength but in the strength of Your Spirit, O God. In Christ our Lord. Amen.

His Heart for Me

Do you have a habit of placing your sins before Him and standing far off thinking that you can't approach your heavenly Father? His arms are wide open welcoming you to Himself. The thought of not being with you in heaven, moved Him to send His Son to the cross. Can you believe that? Speak to the Lord concerning your worth to Him.

Day 5

God Rejoices Over You

The Lord your God is in your midst, A victorious warrior.
He will exult over you with joy, He will be quiet in His love,
He will rejoice over you with shouts of joy.
Zephaniah 3:17

Thought for the Day: The King is enthralled by you; you glisten like gold before Him.

As I strolled to the barn one crisp cold morning to feed our three horses, I had this overwhelming feeling that I was pleasing to the Lord and that He was proud of me. It seemed strange because at the time I felt like I was failing Him in every way possible. I wasn't sharing my faith in Christ with others. Along with the feelings of constant rejection in every area of my life, I felt useless in the Body of Christ.

I was in a wilderness season. We had recently left the church we were attending, and hadn't found a new church yet. My heart was hurting from being disconnected from a church body. I lost sight of my purpose. But with fewer activities, I had more time to spend with the Lord. What seemed like barren land, God turned into fertile soil. It was an amazing time in my life.

As I pondered this thought of how the Lord was pleased with me, I began questioning. *Do I really please You, Lord? Really? Did I hear You right? Aren't You disappointed in me? Everyone else seems to be displeased with me in some way or another.*

The Lord's Heart

From the moment of your conception, I put great thought into the person you were going to be: the color of your eyes, the tone of your voice, your personality, your talents, and your dreams. When you weep, I weep. I know every intimate detail about you. Not a single moment of your life has passed by without Me seeing it and feeling it in the depths of My heart. None of your thoughts, fears, or desires escape Me -- the good, the noble, and the selfless as well as the bad, the selfish, and the prideful. I love you through all of it. I see goodness and beauty within you even when you don't see it in yourself. I rejoice over you with singing like an earthly father who rejoices over his baby's first words or his toddler's first steps. I dance, leap, skip, and shout over you. I take great delight in you by singing. The joyful emotion you bring Me spins Me around happily. You please Me greatly! Rest assured that your Papa in heaven is smiling at you with adoring eyes. I am pleased with you. I am not disappointed in you.

And David was dancing before the Lord with all his might.
2 Samuel 6:14

Declaration

I bring joy to my heavenly Father.

Prayer

Abba Father, I rejoice and give You praise today and every day of my life. May the joy of my salvation and thoughts of living with You in heaven be my garment of praise. If there be any spirit of rejection in my thoughts, prune them now and burn them up. Reveal the gold You see in me and speak to my spirit concerning the things I do that bring You great joy. Holy Spirit, open my eyes to see God smiling upon me from heaven with His eyes sparkling. In Christ our Lord. Amen.

His Heart for Me

Make a joyful noise and spin around to the sound of your praises to Him. Worship without limitation like David did. Without concern for what others thought, David worshipped the Lord in spirit and truth giving glory to the One who deserves all our praise. Take time to visualize Jesus dancing with you. Ask the Lord what He loves about you, those things that cause Him to dance, leap, sing, and shout over you and record it here.

Day 6

How God Speaks

My sheep hear my voice, and I know them, and they follow Me.
John 10:27

Thought for the Day: I can sense the Lord's voice. I can hear Him well in my spirit.

All of God's children can hear His voice. (John 10:4) God calls us His sons and daughters (His sheep) who hear His voice and follow after Him. Jesus calls us His friends, friends have conversations with each other. When your friend calls you on the phone, how do you know it is your friend and not a stranger? For me, I know it is my friend because I have spent time with them. I know the tone of their voice and how they talk, even the pitch of their voice. This is how our relationship with the Lord can be.

God speaks through the Bible, dreams and visions, creation, signs, music, movies, His angels, your prayer time, impressions and sensations in your body, the audible voice of the Lord, a gentle knowing or whisper in your mind, and through your sense of smell.

Hearing the audible voice of God is possible for all of God's children. I once had an encounter similar to Samuel, where the Lord called me by name while I was sleeping. His voice was loud and urgent which led me to believe He had some important instructions for my life. I waited to hear more but nothing more came. The next morning I awoke with so much love and gratitude in my heart for I truly felt known and loved by God.

God speaks to me daily through visions. I receive warnings and encouragement for myself and others through visions. God tends to speak symbolic messages to us in our dreams and usually more literally through visions. If God is speaking to you through dreams and visions, ask the Holy Spirit for wisdom, understanding, and the interpretation, then go write it down. Ask what your responsibility is to what you are seeing.

God speaks to us through His creation and our environment. Owls have stood in front of my car and stared at me. The Lord then spoke, "I am bringing greater discernment to you and increasing your spiritual sight." Another time seven hawks were circling to the south of me and then vanished suddenly. This represented a south wind and molting process occurring in my life. I love it when God speaks to me through nature. Has God spoken to you through nature?

The most common way to hear His voice is through a gentle voice within our spirit. We will often have spontaneous thoughts bubble up in our spirits. Other times you will have impressions or feelings. It is important to remember that we must use discernment when navigating through what we are receiving. We can receive downloads from the Lord, from our souls, and from our enemy. Run everything you receive through a purifying filter and check it against the Word of God.

If you want to hear the voice of God, you need to spend time with Him and get to know Him, just like you do with your friends. Set up a date with Jesus in the midst of your busy schedule and learn to listen, as well as speak. As we learn to recognize the voice of God, He will direct our path.

The Lord's Heart

You were created to know My voice intimately. My Spirit is intertwined with your spirit. My DNA is in you because I am your heavenly Father. I love to listen to your heartfelt prayers, they fill Me with joy. Daily, I have assignments for you. Will you take time to ask Me what those assignments are? Some will be as simple as making your family dinner and serving them in love. As you come to Me, I will reveal great and hidden things that you have not known. Press in a little longer when you are with Me. Don't be in a rush, carve out time to listen to Me.

Whoever is born of Me hears My words. I shall speak to your spirit telling you the way to go and encourage you to walk in it. My Spirit speaks the truth to you and will guide you into all truth. Truly, you are blessed to hear from Me in this way, and even more blessed, if you obey My word. Remember that My words are alive and active; they are spirit and life. Meditate on My words to you, beloved. Incline your ear to Me today. Your good and faithful Shepherd is waiting to not only lead you but speak with you.

But when He, the Spirit of truth, comes, He will guide you into all the truth; for He will not speak on His own initiative, but whatever He hears, He will speak; and He will disclose to you what is to come.
John 16:13

Declaration

The Lord speaks to me.

Prayer

Abba Father, I adore You and thank you for wanting to talk to me. Holy Spirit, open up new ways for me to hear from You. Silence all the chaos and busyness in my mind when I am trying to hear you, Lord. I declare that I will not be jealous of others but passionately pursue my own intimate relationship with Christ and discover how He wants to speak to me specifically. I am open to any way You desire to speak to me. Communicate to me through all my senses. I praise You and give You thanks for loving me so much. In Christ our Lord. Amen.

His Heart for Me

What ways do you hear the Lord most often? Make a list of how He talks to you and thank Him for it. Then ask Him to open up another way of communication between the two of you. Smelling the scent of Christ is amazing. Ask Him to utilize all your senses so you can know Him better.

Day 7

The Great I AM

Therefore, accept one another,
just as Christ also accepted us to the glory of God.
Romans 15:7

Thought for the Day: The great I AM loves and accepts me just the way I am.

What is the first thing we do when hurt or rejected by others? We isolate ourselves, so we won't get hurt again. I have done this many times. When we are resistant to the transformation process in our lives, we withdraw from God and others, those He wants to use to transform us.

We were never made to live in isolation. People who interact with others are far healthier and happier than those who are isolated and lonely. Although relationships can be difficult, God uses others in our lives to sharpen us, to strip away the rough edges, so we can grow and mature.

Relationships often point out the areas where we need growth. God may place you in relationships that bring out the worst in you because He wants to get the yuck out of you for good. How will the yuck get out of you if you keep running from one relationship to another looking for others to be perfect? Some relationships are toxic and need to be severed. And others need to be worked through, so both parties can grow and mature. Our humanity might want others to change, but God wants the heart change to begin with us.

We all want to fit in, to be accepted somewhere, by someone. Many times pleasing people becomes our vehicle to find acceptance. When you are fulfilling everyone's demands as well as the demands you put on yourself but you still aren't accepted by others, then what happens? You become angry, bitter, and feel manipulated. This is where I lived. Since

I couldn't please anyone, it made me feel worthless, rejected, and tired. After spending time with God, I realized that not everyone will like me and He was helping me be okay with that. When I started believing my true worth and acceptance as a daughter of the King, my focus changed from pleasing people to pleasing God above all else. Now I am empowered to love my enemies and say no when necessary. Our true acceptance and affirmation comes from the Lord Jesus, not others.

The Lord's Heart

You are My beloved child. Don't forget how much I love you. You can always find acceptance, grace, and love from Me in all of life's trials. In times of loneliness, I am your true friend who understands. However, I have not called you to a life of loneliness. You are called to have thriving fruitful relationships. You are called to be a light to others. How can you be the light if you are hiding in the darkness away from My people and potential hurt and rejection? Don't let rejection stop you from being that light to others. Rejection is part of the Christian life. I wish to mature you through all your trials and testings. How can I mature you if you avoid difficult people? Difficult relationships are part of My plan to make you more like Christ.

The great I AM surrounds you with songs of acceptance, worth, and love. I will bring peace as you work through the difficult relationships in your life. As you stay submitted to Me, I will stir up joy, love, and harmony in you and those around you. I am preparing to bless you.

And although you were formerly alienated and hostile in mind, engaged in evil deeds, yet He has now reconciled you in His fleshly body through death, in order to present you before Him holy and blameless and beyond reproach.
Colossians 1:21-22

Declaration

I will grow and mature to be more like Christ as I work through the difficult relationships in my life.

Prayer

Abba Father, thank you for loving me with an everlasting love that is not dependent on what I do or don't do. Thank you for Your undeserved love and mercy. Thank you for the relationships in my life that are hard, those relationships that rub me the wrong way. I am grateful that I can always find acceptance and affirmation in Your courts. Holy Spirit, draw me out of isolation and protective behaviors caused by past wounds. Heal my heart and help me to forgive others. Lord, bring revival to my conversations. In Christ our Lord. Amen.

His Heart for Me

Are you waiting to be accepted and loved by those around you in order to feel good about yourself? Do you believe the words that people speak about you more than what the Lord says about you? Have you isolated yourself from others as a form of protection? Are you only comfortable around yourself? Seek Jesus and ask Him where you need to grow. Ask Him to speak to you about how you have been accepted and welcomed in the courts of heaven.

ALL THINGS
Are Possible
Ah, Lord God! Behold, You have made the heavens
and the earth by Your great power and by Your
outstretched arm! Nothing is too difficult for You.
Jeremiah 32:17

Day 8

You Have So Much Potential

For I am confident of this very thing, that He who began a good work in you will perfect it until the day of Christ Jesus.
Philippians 1:6

Thought for the Day: As I stay submitted to Christ, I will reach my full potential.

As I sat in a Christian women's book group, a lady who was typically quiet said to me, "You have so much potential." A puzzled look crossed my face. It was almost as if I didn't hear her the first time. My mind couldn't comprehend her words. She repeated herself, "You have so much potential." It sunk into my heart. I grabbed hold of this small, but powerful, sentence. No one had ever spoken these words to me, quite the opposite actually. This message hit the target. There were many things I wanted to do for the Lord, but didn't feel smart enough to venture out and do them. Now I was willing to try.

Weeks went by as I meditated and wrestled with the thought that I had potential. For most of my life I had been told I wasn't smart and I believed that lie. Barely passing high school solidified that false belief. As a result of this new mindset, I enrolled in an online Bible college knowing that I could do whatever the Lord laid on my heart and do it well because of His strength, not my own. I was shocked by how well I did. I graduated from Bible college because it was God's plan for me. God gave me great confidence in His ability, that's what carried me through. He will do the same for you. Always remember—

You have so much potential!
With God, you will reach your full potential and maturity!

The Lord's Heart

Child, I have placed My plans in your heart. Don't look at your abilities but Mine. With Me, all things are possible! You will be led through many seasons before My purposes are fulfilled. Don't rush ahead of Me to make things happen in your timing. My timing is perfect.

To fulfill My purpose, you will need to be at a certain level of maturity in your walk with Me. Without this wisdom and maturity, you will fall short of My best for you. My plan will fail on your timetable but will succeed on My perfect timetable. I take all things into consideration and see the full scope of My plans for you. The fulfillment of My plans for you will bring great joy in this life.

Many times, your calling and My big plans are kept secret, so you don't run ahead of Me. Submit your will to Me and trust in My will and plans for your life. You have great potential in this life because My Son lives inside of you. You are precious and valuable to Me, says the Lord Almighty!

Now to Him who is able to do far more abundantly beyond all that we ask or think, according to the power that works within us.
Ephesians 3:20

Declaration

I will fulfill all things inscribed about me in heaven.

Prayer

Abba Father, reveal my potential. Give me a fresh awareness that I can do all things through Christ who strengthens me. I pray for a rock solid faith! I declare no lie from the enemy will make me think I am worthless and of no value. Stir up those things I thought I couldn't do because my eyes were on me and not You. Holy Spirit, breathe on all the forgotten and shelved dreams. Bring hope and life to the godly desires within me. You are the way maker, Lord. Make a way for all God-breathed dreams and passions to be fulfilled. In Christ our Lord. Amen.

His Heart for Me

What dreams or passions have you shelved? Why are they shelved? Is God telling you it's time to take one of them off the shelf? Ask the Holy Spirit to reveal the Father's heart concerning your dreams and passions, then pray in faith and pray big prayers. Grab that cup of coffee or tea and envision Jesus sitting with you, speaking all that is in your heavenly book.

Day 9

Secure and Confident

Therefore let us draw near to the throne of grace, so that we may receive mercy and find grace to help in time of need.
Hebrews 4:16

Thought for the Day: Sanctification is an ongoing, purifying process; a life of holiness God works in us for His good pleasure.

Competition, perfectionism, and insecurity will always lead us to compare ourselves to others. When we do this, we are acting foolishly and without understanding. Be free from thinking less of yourself because your eyes are on another person's gifting. Some have pity parties for themselves, while others doubt God's goodness towards them. Ask God to forgive you and help you view yourself through His eyes. Freedom comes when we receive a fresh revelation about how much He loves us and who He made us to be. A new healthy love for ourselves is what we need!

The only thing that matters is what God thinks about us. As believers in Christ, we are on the trail called "Sanctification." There will be many stops along the way. The places we stop are where God will help us work through areas that need more time and attention. Be patient with yourself during your time of spiritual growth.

God uses our trials to help us overcome our weaknesses. We must use Christ as our example. Each believer is at a different place in the transformation process of becoming more like Christ. When you see a believer more advanced in a specific area, don't believe the lie that they are more special than you. You may be further along in becoming more Christ-like in another area. Do not condemn or criticize your brother or sister for not being where you are.

There will be moments on our transformation journey, when we long to see the finished product. When we want to hear, "Well-done, good and faithful servant" and know that our lives are pleasing to the Lord, but God is just as interested in the process as He is the outcome. There are great blessings even in our suffering, that cause His glory to be manifested in us. Be willing and patient for God to complete His good work in you.

The Lord's Heart

All My children are anointed according to the grace that I have given each one. Some have been given more grace than you in certain areas. To each of My children I have given a measure of faith and grace. Practice and exercise what I have called you to do instead of worrying if you are as good as someone else. Be confident in who I have created you to be, My child. Stop looking at others. Rest assured that I will finish the good work I started in you, in all My children, for My good pleasure. Trust Me, I know what I am doing. The great and mighty I AM is holding your hand as you stroll down the trail called sanctification. My angels will hold you up and keep your feet from falling. Don't attempt to rush ahead and avoid all your predestined stops. Enjoy the hike knowing that I will never leave you or forsake you. Walking with Me is an intense spiritual pursuit of connection and friendship. I desire a daily walking relationship with you. You will walk with Me in the cool of the day just as I walked with Adam and Eve. Come, let us walk and talk together.

For You formed my inward parts; You wove me in my mother's womb. I will give thanks to You, for I am fearfully and wonderfully made; Wonderful are Your works, And my soul knows it very well.

Psalm 139:13-14

Declaration

I will no longer compare myself to others.

Prayer

Abba Father, may I find my true identity and security in You. I shall learn to be comfortable in my own skin and appreciate who You made me to be. For I am captivating, unique, and highly adored by You. At Your feet, I drop my perfectionism and competitive ways. Holy Spirit, empower me to value and honor others, and the grace you have placed upon their lives. May I rejoice with others when they accomplish things for You instead of being jealous. Jealousy, envy, and strife, be far removed from me! I will cast down vain imaginations and seek what is pure and holy.

In Christ our Lord. Amen.

His Heart for Me

Do you look at someone else's accomplishments and think badly about yourself or do you criticize others so you feel better about yourself? Seek His heart and ask God to help you be secure in who you are, secure in who He made you to be. You are unique, and He has specific assignments only you can fulfill. Throw off comparing yourself to others. Write down what the Lord loves about you.

Day 10

Sowing and Reaping

I planted, Apollos watered, but God was causing the growth. So then neither the one who plants nor the one who waters is anything, but God who causes the growth. Now he who plants and he who waters are one; but each will receive his own reward according to his own labor.
1 Corinthians 3:6-8

Thought for the Day: What you sow into the lives of others is the harvest you will reap tomorrow. If you don't like what you are reaping, change what you are sowing.

The parable of sowing and reaping is like gardening. Our lives are like gardens and every day we are sowing seeds whether we realize it or not. What are the seeds we are planting in our gardens? Our words, thoughts, and actions are the seeds we plant every day. Whatever comes out of your mouth was first sowed in your mind and heart. Are your seeds positive and life-giving or negative and death-producing? When we listen to others speak, their words will indicate the kind of seeds that have been sown in the garden of their hearts.

I have had some unpleasant experiences that have cemented this lesson in my heart. Christians from well-known ministries have called to ask if they could pray for me. I was shocked by their request. The wow factor and hook that caught me was the fact that they showed care and concern, and also prayed for exactly what we needed. Towards the end of the conversation, they started talking about sowing and reaping. They said things like: "You will reap a mighty harvest if you will sow one thousand dollars into this ministry. Don't miss out on what God wants to reap in your life because you aren't sowing." At that time, my husband and I were sowing into several other ministries and missions. The pressure to sow one thousand dollars was enormous and they really weren't accepting of any other dollar amount.

The Lord had been increasing my discernment and I was getting wiser about deceitful people, after being deceived far too many times. I told the man on the phone that I only listen to where God wants me to sow and He wasn't telling me to sow into this ministry. The pressure continued. "Didn't I just pray an amazing prayer over you? You really needed that prayer and it touched you greatly, won't you bless us for that powerful prayer?"

Wow, prayer costs money now?

The Lord quickly spoke to me: *They accessed My spiritual realm, not through a pure relationship with Me, but through greed. I will bless you because I love you and prayer should always be free. Hang up.*

Jesus is the Master Gardener. Seek His wisdom and He will answer. We must listen to His voice and sow our financial seed where He directs us. Our words, thoughts, and actions will also need the Master Gardener's touch so the seeds in our own gardens will grow into beautiful plants that produce an abundant harvest. May our gardens grow without weeds.

The Lord's Heart

The godly seeds that have been planted in your heart, I will cause to grow! The prophecies you have been given from heaven concerning your future shall not lie dormant. The seeds shall be fertilized and watered. You do the fertilizing by reading My written word. I'll do the watering and bring the seeds to fruition by lining up the circumstances around you. Others will come to you and water those seeds with hope and faith. Keep believing in the visions, dreams, and words that have been spoken over you, mull them over occasionally. Have faith that I will bring those seeds to fruition.

Many of the visions I have shown you concerning your future seem too large or impossible. It is good to understand that without Me you can't fulfill My purposes for your life. Remember that I am the God of impossibilities. With Me, nothing is impossible. Do you lack in finances? I will bless you with unexpected finances including making money stretch and last longer than normal. Have you always wanted to preach the word with signs and wonders? Seek a relationship with Me and that will fall into place. Don't seek the signs and wonders, seek Me. Remember to sow seeds of hope into your life instead of doubt. Be careful what you sow and to whom you sow, dear children. Sow truth and life into the lives of your family. Sow righteousness and stay in faith and you shall reap a mighty reward. The great I AM will reward you for doing the right thing even if a wrong thing is happening.

Sow with a view to righteousness, Reap in accordance with kindness; Break up your fallow ground, For it is the time to seek the Lord Until He comes to rain righteousness on you.
Hosea 10:12

Declaration

I will sow generously in word and deed,
then I shall reap a harvest for the kingdom of God.

Prayer

Abba Father, I ask for Your wisdom to know where to sow the money You have blessed me with. Let my eyes be open to deceitful and greedy people serving their own desires. Rain Your favor and grace upon me. Thank you for providing what I need and not always what I want. Holy Spirit, help me to be content with what I have and be a good steward of it all. May the seeds of my mouth be clean and line up with Your will and life plan for me and others. I will be faithful to fertilize my mind and seeds by reading Your holy words to me in the best book in the world, the Bible.

In Christ our Lord. Amen.

His Heart for Me

Write down what you are currently sowing in finances, in words, and deeds. If you don't like what you are reaping, look at what you are sowing on a regular basis. Are you reaping stress and negativity or are you reaping peace and joy? Have you sown seeds of doubt? Pursue the Lord and His ideas regarding what you are to be sowing.

Day 11

Justified by Faith

It was for freedom that Christ set us free; therefore keep standing firm and do not be subject again to a yoke of slavery.
Galatians 5:1

Thought for the Day: Hold fast to your liberty in Christ.

As believers, we have freedom in Christ. Early in our walk of faith, my husband and I had our freedom stolen by our lack of scriptural knowledge. We started out in the Spirit but fell into foolishness. A year after being saved, we were no longer walking by faith, but by works and obedience to the law of the Old Testament.

While my husband was in nursing school, there was a friend he met with often. They would share their faith and his friend shared all the rules that he kept as a Christian. Rules we weren't keeping, thus making us feel guilty and condemned. These rules consisted of keeping the Sabbath faithfully, including a list of rules of what you couldn't do including no cooking, no wearing bathing suits or going swimming, and many others. This did not sit well with me. I fought hard against all of these rules for a time knowing that it was just not right. Eventually I gave up the fight and believed the lie from satan that if I didn't keep them, then I wasn't pleasing to God and I wasn't saved.

With each month at this church, we felt more condemned. We tried hard to keep all the rules but never felt like we measured up. We certainly didn't feel loved by the Father. It took a few years for us to be healed of all this legalism. And many more years to be healed of our so-called righteous judgment of others who didn't follow "the rules." Not only did we feel condemned, but we condemned others and judged harshly.

Towards the last month before we left the church, I started questioning why we never read out of the book of Hebrews. As I read Hebrews, I understood why. Hebrews is a book about Christ and how He set us free from rule keeping. It is the book that set me free from legalism and set me back on the path of faith in Christ.

The more I tried to obey, to follow the rules, the more I failed. The good news is we have help on this journey. God helps us to become more like Christ every day as we surrender and seek His face and His ways of living. We are accepted not by what we do, or don't do, but by our repentant hearts and Christ's sacrifice. A deeper relationship with Christ and trusting Him to make you all He wants you to be is the path to freedom. Faith in Christ makes you approved and accepted, plain and simple! The Holy Spirit will transform you and teach you how to live righteously and free. Before long you will be obeying all God wants you to without even noticing or trying. Obedience will be your first inclination without a man-made rule book. We are free in Christ, not free to sin, but free to live.

The Lord's Heart

I have made a new covenant with you through Christ Jesus. This new covenant is better than the first. The first covenant I made with My people was a simple way of making My ways known. A way of teaching them what pleases Me and what doesn't. They couldn't fulfill My laws then and you can't fulfill My ways now. I needed to send My Son, the ultimate sacrifice to cover all the sins of My people once and for all. Truly when someone repents for their sinful ways it is covered and washed away by the blood of My Son. You no longer have to try to obey every command on your own for My laws are written on your heart and My Spirit will enable you to obey Me. Obedience will come not in your own strength but in the strength of My Son and in the power of His blood that was shed for you. If you love Me with all your heart, you will obey Me without even thinking about it. You won't need to keep a record of wrongs or things to do or not to do.

If you seek a relationship with Me and let go of trying to fulfill the law, I will come and inhabit your heart and truly teach you what is pleasing to Me and what is not. I created the Sabbath for man, so you could rest from your work. I created it because I know what is good for you. You can choose to not observe a day of rest, that will not disqualify you from salvation. But it would do you great good to observe a day of rest and spend time with Me as I bring you refreshment from your work week. Remember, My plans for you are better than your own. I love you, your Papa above.

But now He has obtained a more excellent ministry, by as much as He is also the mediator of a better covenant, which has been enacted on better promises. For if that first covenant had been faultless, there would have been no occasion sought for a second.
Hebrews 8:6-7

Declaration

I will hold tight to the freedom Christ won for me at the cross.

Prayer

Abba Father, may we hold fast to the freedom we have been granted through Christ Jesus. I will not be yoked and enslaved again to the law. Thank you for giving us Your Spirit who helps us to obey and live a life that is pleasing to You without being so focused on just obeying the rules. When we love You, we will walk in obedience. Holy Spirit, break off every yoke holding us hostage to the law. We praise You for redeeming us from the curse of the law and bringing us into the tabernacle of grace.

In Christ our Lord. Amen.

His Heart for Me

Do you ever feel approved and accepted by God because of what you do? Maybe you feed the poor or do other charitable deeds, do you feel this qualifies you? You are approved and accepted only by accepting Christ Jesus' sacrifice for your sins. Salvation is a free gift through faith, you can't earn it! Ask the Lord for more understanding concerning your true acceptance in Him if you find yourself feeling accepted only by the things you do.

Day 12

Never Just a Mom

Come to Me, all who are weary and heavy-laden, and I will give you rest.
Matthew 11:28

Thought for the Day: The time I spend with my children is important.

"I am just a mom, a stay at home mom who homeschools." This was my response when asked what I did for a living. I always left feeling bad about myself after answering that question. My focus needed to be adjusted. Our job as mothers is one of the hardest things we'll ever do, but also the most rewarding.

Jesus had 12 disciples who were like His "children." Christ poured His life into these twelve, by feeding them love, patience, and kindness every single day. When Christ showed compassion to others, He was giving us an example of how to love our children. Smile and give your children hugs. Love them while you still have them in your home. Remind them you will always love them regardless of their grades, hair color, or the poor choices they will inevitably make. When they move out, continue to shower them with love through text messages, calls, or lunch dates.

When Jesus washed His disciples' feet, He was showing them great humility. (John 13:1-17) They were dirty from walking all day and Jesus didn't flinch at the dirt. As parents, we get dirty too. Years ago when we were traveling with our 8-month-old daughter, I was feeding her in the car to keep her happy and she threw up all over me. We had many miles to go and I didn't smell very good. Both my daughter and I were uncomfortable but it didn't diminish my love for her. Jesus served His disciples with great love and without any grumbling. Do the same thing toward your family and others.

During the training years, we can get tired. Sometimes we believe we aren't making a difference or that our children just aren't "getting it." Jesus showed a bit of frustration with His disciples when He said, "How much longer must I be with you?" (Mark 9:19) Many times, Jesus asks, "Do you still not understand?" (Matthew 16:9) Jesus got frustrated with their lack of understanding and we do, too, with our children's lack of understanding and listening skills. Daily I need much grace and patience. I fail often, ask forgiveness often, and keep on pressing into Jesus, my example. He gives me all that I need if I will seek Him diligently.

Parents, Jesus understands our lack of quiet time, time to spend alone with Him. People followed Jesus everywhere He went. When John the Baptist died, Jesus wanted to be alone and talk to God (Matthew 14:13). When Jesus heard the news, He got in a boat and went to a remote area to be alone, but the crowds followed Him. Jesus needed to be comforted by His Father and refreshed in His presence.

There are many ways that our loving Father will refresh us, if we take the time. Jesus had to get away late at night or very early in the morning when people were still sleeping to have His quiet time. Sound familiar? Sometimes your trip to the bathroom or shower is your only time to be with Jesus. Jesus understands. He doesn't say, "You should be doing more." Instead He says, "Hello, My child, I'm glad you are here." Jesus knew the importance of spending time with God and He is God's Son. Even a few minutes in the morning before your children wake up does wonders for your day. I learned to pray and talk to God while I was doing the dishes and folding the laundry. When I made this my habit, it gave me more patience and kindness throughout the day.

Remember, you are not "just a mom or dad." You are dearly loved by your heavenly Father. Weary parent, in His presence, you will find peace of mind and refreshing for your soul.

The Lord's Heart

Dearly beloved parents, your job is very important. You are raising the next generation that will serve and love Me. Mothers and fathers, you have a high calling and a great responsibility. Reject any thoughts that say your job doesn't matter for it does and the rewards in heaven will be great.

Do you know that you are representing the great I AM to your children by your words and actions every single day? You are sowing many seeds through your loving, serving, and teaching. Be quick to apologize to your children when needed. As you humble yourself, you will raise humble and forgiving children. Your children will reflect the example you were to them during those years in your home. Even if they turn away for a time, I will bring them back to the ways you taught them. If you need rest from it all, ask Me to refresh you and I will, My child. Precious parents, remember to take care of yourselves, it's important.

Your child-rearing years will make you more like Christ. Parenting is the wildest roller coaster you'll ever ride with many ups and downs and sharp unexpected turns along the way. Buckle up and hold on tight to Me.

But we proved to be gentle among you, as a nursing mother tenderly cares for her own children. Having so fond an affection for you, we were well-pleased to impart to you not only the gospel of God but also our own lives, because you had become very dear to us.
1 Thessalonians 2:7-8

Declaration

I am earning eternal rewards through parenting.

Prayer

Abba Father, empower me to be the best representative of Christ that I can be to my children. Keep me humble and repentant. Your patience and kindness I shall wear like a coat, daily. I declare that I will give my children quality time uninterrupted by cell phones and television. Thank you for Your constant wisdom and understanding during these child-rearing years. Holy Spirit, enable me to love, honor, and respect my children. Give me the eyes to see all the good You have deposited in them. I will seek to be my child's greatest support system. Heal any communication problems within my relationships with my children. In Christ our Lord. Amen.

His Heart for Me

One of the greatest gifts we can give our children is our time and attention. When we spend time with them, we are telling our children we love them and think they are important. Your perseverance will pay off, don't give up. What can you do today to show your children you love them unconditionally? What is their love language? Record your course of action, inspired by Christ, in showing your love to them.

Day 13

Do You Care What Others Think?

By this all men will know that you are My disciples,
if you have love for one another.
John 13:35

Thought for the Day: Trying to please people will only bring stress, frustration, and misery to your life. Just be who God created you to be.

Those who declare that they don't care what others think are the ones that care the most. They wish they didn't, but they do. One day while standing in the checkout line at the grocery store, my 16-year-old daughter and I overheard the man in front of us cussing and making inappropriate sexual comments. He was declaring loudly, that he didn't care what others thought of him and added some more graphic language. My face turned red, as I laughed uncomfortably. I'm rarely around people who behave in this fashion and very quickly I can get quite embarrassed and disgusted. The disgust left me as God reminded me of His heart towards all His children, that is, those who know and love Him, and those who don't. I wish I had told this man who was cussing what I saw because it was beautiful! I saw that he had a tender and compassionate heart. His very loving heart had been hurt by others which caused him to put up walls of protection.

While heading out to our car, the man approached us and apologized for his behavior and said he had a habit of "saying things like it is." I told him, "I heard" and laughed it off, wishing him a great evening. My daughter and I sat in the car, and almost in unison, said, "So, he does care what we think!"

Should we care what others think of us?

My goal in life is to keep my focus on God and what is pleasing to Him. Others won't always like me, I'm okay with that. I am here representing Christ to the world. When others who know me are saying unkind things about me, I ask the Lord, "What's the truth? Do I need to repent or change anything?" God is always faithful to show us the error of our ways and the lies of others, if we are willing to listen. We must live to please God and not man. God wants to use us to draw others closer to Him. Show kindness to those who are different than you. Only by the grace of God can we recognize the gold in others. Let's not miss any God opportunities.

The Lord's Heart

You are My representatives on earth. When others know you are a Christian, and they don't know Me, it is extremely important how you reflect My love. As you navigate through the tough circumstances and relationships in your life, others see how you face the storms of life with hope and great joy. Their lives are measured against yours, and you have something they need. Share how it is that you have peace and you will draw them to Me, the Lamb of God. The lost people in this world will know you have been with Me because of the words you speak and the love you show. Your actions truly do speak louder than your words. Be a doer of My written word. Be faithful in demonstrating My love to others. You are My ambassadors on earth.

Ask Me to show you the gold, the good, and lovely things in others. Then step out in confidence and faith to reveal it to that precious one in front of you regardless of their current behavior. Your words, inspired by Me, will cut through all their defense mechanisms and touch the core of their heart for Me. A seed of truth will be planted. A seed I will continue to water throughout their lives.

Whatever you do in word or deed, do all in the name of the Lord Jesus, giving thanks through Him to God the Father.
Colossians 3:17

Declaration

I will seek to please the Lord and only Him.

Prayer

Abba Father, I shall seek to please and obey You all the days of my life. I declare that I will put Jesus on display everywhere I go, glorifying Him in all I do. I will choose to respect and honor others even if their behavior is despicable. When others experience the love of Christ, they will be moved to apologize and repent in their own way. Holy Spirit, abundantly display all Your fruit and power in my life to influence others, for the gospel preached without power and love is not the true gospel of Jesus Christ. Lord, pour out Your Spirit on me in greater abundance so that You will be glorified. In Christ our Lord. Amen.

His Heart for Me

Who are you in the habit of pleasing? Do you seek to please yourself, others, or God? How can you represent Christ better to your family and friends? What would He have you do? Ask the Lord to show you the one who is ready to receive Him as their savior and speak to them in love and boldness. He will be with your mouth. We don't want to focus on works, but our faith will move us to demonstrate His love as we represent Christ well to those around us.

Day 14

Revival Begins With You And Me

Create in me a clean heart, O God,
And renew a steadfast spirit within me.
Psalm 51:10

Thought for the Day: Revival starts with me as I lean into the transforming work of Christ through repentance.

Revival seems to be the word on every Christian's tongue these days. Many people say we need revival because they are looking at others and the condition of our world, and nation. However, they forget to look at themselves. What is your spiritual condition? Is it dry and religious? Do you have a form of godliness but feel God is far away? Do you know you can meet with Jesus every day? Jesus wants to have a living relationship with you, one in which you communicate with Him and listen to Him every day of your life. Are you hungry for more of Jesus? I am! Our hearts need to turn back toward God. We need to stay awake to our responsibilities as royal priests in His Kingdom.

Many Christians are hindering revival in their own lives by their constant declaration of being sinners and worms in the dust. Don't take swings at your identity in Christ! Your sin nature was buried with Christ. We will occasionally sin, but repent and move on. Meditate on the fact that now you are a saint and child of God. You have a responsibility to continue the work of Christ by sharing the gospel, making disciples, and putting the power of the Holy Spirit on display through exercising the gifts of the Holy Spirit.

I was once a complacent and comfortable Christian. Going to church on Sunday and praying a few minutes a day were enough for me. God shook me out of my complacency by putting a passion in my heart to be about His business. Today I am an "uncomfortable" Christian. God has taken me way outside my comfort zone for the sake of His Kingdom and His glory.

The Lord says that as we seek Him, He will draw near to us. (James 4:8) Revival can break out in your house and heart every time you wholeheartedly seek Him. Humbly ask Him to fill you with more of His likeness. God will happily answer your request.

Don't wait for the next revival to break out somewhere else. Seek Him now in your own quiet time and be willing to let Him have His way in your life today. You will bring revival to others as you share what God has done for you.

The Lord's Heart

I am bringing revival to Christian homes around the world. My sword comes to divide and divide rightly. My Spirit will convict My people to be righteousness and call them to holy living. As My Spirit turns up the heat, scales will be removed from many blind eyes and blankets from many minds bringing fresh understanding and clarity. The devil will lose his access points to My children. I am opening the eyes of My children in greater numbers than ever before. Those who belong to Me will recognize the source of their problems. My children will be able to divide the truth from a lie. They will be able to discern the actions of the enemy in another person and still love them. My children will forgive quickly because they want nothing to hinder our relationship. Those who believe in Me, but don't understand that there are evil forces trying to hinder them, will have greater discernment. They will learn to be as wise as serpents to the schemes of the devil and as innocent as doves. I will teach them to be Jesus-focused instead of devil-focused. My children shall rise to a higher level of understanding as they grow in their relationship with Me. As My children truly know Me and My ways, they will walk in a constant state of revival. They will choose to stay on the path of life called: My will.

The great I AM is shaking things up and breaking up the fallow ground. Revival starts with you, My precious one. Then it will spread to others. Pride and greed quench My Spirit so come humbly before My throne and I will bring that revival into your heart today. New life will spring up in the dry and weathered places in your life. Pursue Me more than the things of this world.

The law of the Lord is perfect, restoring the soul;
The testimony of the Lord is sure, making wise the simple.
Psalm 19:7

Prayer

Abba Father, I humbly ask for more of You today. I repent for all my ways that are not pleasing to You including my pride and arrogance. I repent for loving the things of this world more than loving You. Come into my heart and make Your home there. May my heart be pleasing to You so You want to stay there forever. Holy Spirit, I open myself to Your constant reviving work. I yield fully to what You want to do in my life. May true revival be mine all the days of my life. I shall never grow weary of seeking Your face.

In Christ our Lord. Amen.

Declaration

Everything within me will seek the Lord.

His Heart for Me

Do you need restoration? Are you worn out and tired? Is God the most important thing in your life or has He gotten pushed out by something else? Do you need improvement or rejuvenation in your relationship with Jesus? Let's return to our first love and seek His face in confidence and humility.

___

___

___

HOLY

In His Sight

Yet He has now reconciled you in His fleshly body
through death, in order to present you before Him
holy and blameless and beyond reproach.

Colossians 1:22

Day 15

Rising Above the Offense

Let all bitterness and wrath and anger and clamor and slander be put away from you, along with all malice. Be kind to one another, tender-hearted, forgiving each other, just as God in Christ also has forgiven you.
Ephesians 4:31-32

Thought for the Day: The truth is, what offends you, reveals you. —Brant Hansen

---

Jesus warned us that offenses would come in the last days. It's what we do about them that matters. God knows that if an offense comes your way, it will reveal if there is an area in your heart where forgiveness is needed. Those who struggle with rejection will become more prone to being offended because they view life through a negative lens. They believe people are always against them. This broken-heartedness keeps them open to the voices of offense, bitterness, and unforgiveness.

In Matthew 15:21-28, we read the story of a woman who refused to be offended by the words of others. "A Canaanite woman from that region [the district of Tyre and Sidon] came out and began to cry out, saying, "Have mercy on me, Lord, Son of David; my daughter is cruelly demon-possessed." Jesus does not answer one word of this woman's cry while His disciples are trying to get rid of her because she's causing a commotion. When Jesus does respond, He says, "I was sent only to the lost sheep in the house of Israel." (Meaning: The Jews and not the Gentiles.) This Canaanite woman does not give up. She comes and bows down before Jesus saying, "Lord, help me!"

This mother's eyes are glued on Jesus not paying any attention to the dirty looks of those around her. Her daughter's life depended on Jesus helping her. In reply to her second plea, Jesus says, "It is not good to take the children's bread and throw it to the dogs." (Meaning: Why should I give to you what belongs to the Jews?) Can you imagine hearing this from Jesus? The Gentiles were commonly referred to as dogs by the Jewish people. She still doesn't take offense. Instead the woman replies, "Yes, Lord, but even the dogs feed on the crumbs which fall from their master's table." (Meaning: Jesus' gift of healing is for everyone who believes, Gentile or Jew.) Jesus grants this woman her request; her daughter was healed and delivered. This mother received praise for her great faith.

As Jesus often did, there was a dual lesson at work here, testing not only this woman's heart condition but also His own disciples. This woman's humility and great faith were exposed as was Jesus' disciples lack of patience, kindness, and compassion toward this woman. This mother was desperate for her daughter to be set free. Although there were several opportunities to become offended, she took no offense. Instead, pressing into Jesus, this mother received her heart's deepest desire, her daughter was healed and delivered.

How would you respond if the Lord ignored your cry for help and then told you He only came to help the lost Jews? My response might have been different than hers. Instead of being offended, the Canaanite woman essentially begged the Lord for her daughter's healing. This mother didn't care what she looked like and thought nothing of herself. We are to intercede with this same intensity for our family and friends. May the Lord help us to rise above the perceived offenses in our lives as we pursue His love, healing, and righteousness.

The Lord's Heart

I desire reconciliation between you and your brothers and sisters. You were created to have close relationships so work out your differences and care for each other. Oh, how I wish you would cast down those offenses that come from presumptions and rash judgments. Offenses will come to you, and by you, for this is part of your fallen nature. Choose to give up your rights to be offended. Let go of your retaliation mindset and seek to bless those who persecute you. Ask Me to forgive them just like My Son asked Me to forgive those who killed Him. Jesus asked that I not hold their sins against them. This request released My grace and provided a way for them to realize their sin and repent. Do the same for those who hurt you and I will open that door of adoption through repentance to them as well.

Every time you try to sweep an offense under the rug, it will turn into unforgiveness and bitterness. If you have something against another or someone has something against you, go to them and try to reconcile. Bring the offense out into the open and give the offender an opportunity to apologize. Forgiveness is the best choice, not because you feel like it, but because I have commanded you to forgive others, whether they apologize or not. You can't forgive a wrong done against you in your own strength. Ask for the empowerment of My Spirit as you seek to walk an unoffendable life with Me. Let go of all your rights to be offended, My child. I am the righteous judge, you are not. I will hold people accountable for their actions, that is not your job. Perceived offenses are an opportunity to grow in relationship with Me because it will expose needed areas of growth.

And this I pray, that your love may abound still more and more in real knowledge and all discernment, so that you may approve the things that are excellent, in order to be sincere and blameless until the day of Christ.
Philippians 1:9-10

Declaration

I will choose to not be offended.

Prayer

Abba Father, forgive me for being offended and purify my heart now from all offenses. Holy Spirit, empower me to live my life with no offenses. Perfect me in Your love and help me to forgive quickly. I declare that I shall work through all my offenses in maturity and love for everyone, with the help of the Holy Spirit. Teach me to pray for those who hurt me, to do good to them. Mercy and grace will be the garment I wear constantly. As I walk a life of forgiveness, I will be walking a life of freedom and peace.

In Christ our Lord. Amen.

His Heart for Me

Are you easily offended? Do you try to ignore the wrongs done against you? I encourage you regularly to get out your pen and write down what offends you. Take these things to the Lord and ask Him to reveal the root cause of why these things offend you so much. Ask Him to help you forgive, and bring heart healing and deliverance from the things that cause you to be offended.

Day 16

The Comparison Tug of War

I will give thanks to You, for I am fearfully and wonderfully made;
Wonderful are Your works, And my soul knows it very well.
Psalm 139:14

Thought for the Day: Comparison is the thief of joy.
—Theodore Roosevelt

Comparing ourselves to others is born out of insecurity, competition, and perfectionism. God starting showing me how I was comparing myself to others resulting in feelings of inferiority. Whenever superiority started rising in me, quickly I remembered that superiority is a form of pride and I would repent, knowing that pride is disgusting to the Lord. Being blinded to my true identity in Christ caused me to have a "less than kind" mindset about myself.

We can also compare out of a competitive and perfectionist mindset. I was my own worst critic for many years, ridiculing myself for not living up to God's standard and ridiculing others as well. They didn't know I was doing it. I was having an internal dialogue with God, much like the parable in Luke 18. Our job is to love others and let Jesus be the righteous judge.

When we are caught in this comparison tug of war, we will either feel inferior or superior. In Luke 18, Jesus tells a parable about a Pharisee and a tax collector going to the temple to pray. The Pharisee prayed this prayer: "God, I thank you that I am not like other people: swindlers, unjust, adulterers or even like this tax collector." When the Pharisee looked at the tax collector, he saw a traitor, one who cheated others and helped the Romans. This Pharisee felt superior because he looked at his own actions, how he fasted and tithed, and believed he was more righteous.

What would this look like in our society today? You are in church, worshipping and praising the Lord, and in walks a known prostitute. She starts to worship and praise the Lord. What is your response? Will you judge her praise and worship, wondering if it is pure and acceptable to God? Will you usher her out of your church? My hope is that you would put an arm around her and together rejoice in God's great love and mercy. It's an opportunity to speak life and hope, so she knows the truth about who she is in Christ.

The ground is level at the foot of the cross. There is no place for comparison for we were once sinners, now saints, saved by grace through the death of Jesus Christ.

The Lord's Heart

Compare not, beloved. Oh, how I wish you would not compare yourselves to others. I have made only one of you. You are unique, like none other. Each child is given My grace to soar in their giftings, not someone else's giftings. Why do you look at your brother or sister's giftings and think, "I wish I could do that?" Are you forgetting the many ways I have blessed you? Comparing yourself to others is the quickest way to deactivate that which I have placed in you. The gifts and callings I give you are irrevocable, but they can lie dormant for a lifetime. Comparing can lead to the sin of envy or pride. My dearest child, turn your eyes towards Me. The only one you are to imitate is Jesus Christ. I give you power to be like Him. Count your blessings, beloved, and rejoice in the fact that I have anointed you for a specific purpose that only you can fill exactly how I desire.

Because of your unique experiences, personality, and sufferings, you can reach a specific group of people with the message I have planted in your heart. When you look at another and compare out of insecurity you unknowingly keep yourself in the pit called, "not good enough." Sometimes you compare and look at the faults of others, thinking too highly of yourself. This, too, is born out of insecurity and can lead to pride and destruction. Compare not in any way, My beloved child.

For we are not bold to class or compare ourselves with some of those who commend themselves; but when they measure themselves by themselves and compare themselves with themselves, they are without understanding.
2 Corinthians 10:12

Declaration

From this day forward, I am free from comparing myself to others.

Prayer

Abba Father, tap my shoulder when I start comparing myself to others. May an enormous light bulb go off alerting me to this destructive behavior. I thank you for the strength and power of the Holy Spirit to break this cycle of comparison in my life. Reveal my true identity even more today so that I can fully appreciate who You have created me to be. Give me a new healthy love for myself, because out of loving myself, I will be able to love my neighbors. I declare that I will have a thankful heart that fully appreciates how different we all are from each other. Holy Spirit, give me Jesus' perspective about who I am and who others are.

In Christ our Lord. Amen.

His Heart for Me

When you compare do you feel inferior or superior? If you find yourself feeling superior, repent of your pride. Ask God to show you why you think you are better than others. Do you feel inferior? Ask the Lord to help you appreciate who He has made you to be. Seek the Lord concerning the thief of comparison. He will help you demolish this robber of joy.

Day 17

The Tongue of the Wise

A soothing tongue is a tree of life, But perversion in it crushes the spirit.
Proverbs 15:4

Thought for the Day: You have the mind of Christ. Thinking His thoughts continually is our highest goal and attainable through the power of the Holy Spirit.

Sticking my foot in my mouth has been a habit of mine since my teenage years. Negative thoughts followed me throughout the day. My thought life was on a diet that consisted of past offenses, hurts, and the things I didn't like about others as well as myself. Yes, I was prideful and thought I was better than everyone else (that's a mindset that will always get you in trouble). What we think about comes out of our mouths when we least expect it. Once the word flies out of your mouth, you can't put it back like it was never spoken. If that were possible, I would have tried it on many occasions. After my words hurt a close friend, I finally acknowledged that I needed God's help to tame my tongue and transform my thinking.

Our negative internal thoughts cause great damage to our body, mind, and relationships. The only way our thought life and tongue will be pleasing to the Lord is through a transforming work in our hearts. "As a man thinketh in his heart, so is he." (Proverbs 23:7) We must first fill our heart and mind with God's truth. Make daily declarations of truth. Instead of allowing the devil to win the battle for control of our mind and our words, we must submit ourselves to God for a transforming work that will bear much fruit in our lives.

The Lord's Heart

Dearly beloved, ask Me to sharpen your tongue in speaking blessings and life instead of criticism, judgment, or death. The Holy Spirit living in you releases the power to fill your conversations with grace, life, and compassion. I desire you to speak words of edification, words that lift others up and not words that tear down or wound. You are righteous and wise through Christ, My Son. Weigh your answers and pause before you speak. May the fruit of self-control be evident in your life.

Don't be surprised when offenses come. Bring every offense and hurt to Me, don't run to others. I will help you separate the truth from the lies, the facts from the emotions, so you can see the truth clearly and live a life free of lingering offenses and unhindered intimacy with Me. By sharing your offenses specifically, you gather others who share similar offenses concerning this person creating even greater division. Don't join satan's army of faultfinders. Drop the case and forgive! I dropped your case! Bless them and realize, all are imperfect. There was only one who was pleasing to Me in everything and that was My precious Son, Christ.

If I have allowed you to see an area of weakness in your brother or sister, I revealed it so you would pray. Many times, the faults you see in others are hidden areas of weakness in your own life. Be open to looking at your own areas of weakness and repent. Seek My wisdom and understanding, it is pure and undefiled. My wisdom is peaceable, gentle, reasonable, and full of mercy. Let the righteousness of Christ dwell richly in your hearts. Christ is that life-giving stream that flows within you and out of you. Let it flow and praise Him with your mouth continually.

There is one who speaks rashly like the thrusts of a sword,
But the tongue of the wise brings healing.
Proverbs 12:18

Declaration

I will speak in a way that builds others up.

Prayer

Abba Father, set a guard over my mouth to speak blessings only. Tame my tongue. May my words bring life and nourishment to others. I declare that I will speak words that build up my brothers and sisters. Jealousy and comparison be removed and cast into the sea! Holy Spirit, press upon my heart to forgive and let go of all my offenses. Keep me humble in all my ways, O Lord. I do not want to be rejected by You because of my pride. Give me a pure heart and clean hands so I may stand on Your holy mountain with You. In Christ our Lord. Amen.

His Heart for Me

Do your words bring life to others or do you speak negatively against those the Lord loves? Do you point out the dirt or the gold in others? Ask the Lord for the answers to these questions. Holy Spirit will help you spot the gold in others, if you ask Him. Declaring people's gold to them is fun, you should try it. Record the gold the Lord reveals here.

Day 18

Unresolved Anger

For the anger of man does not achieve the righteousness of God.
James 1:20

Thought for the Day: Don't wait for the feelings to come before you forgive. Forgive first and let God work out your emotions and feelings.

Every time I turn on the television, within moments I wonder why I even bother. Too often the shows that fill our homes depict violent, angry people taking out their revenge on others. This is called entertainment? No wonder road rage is such a problem when our families are feeding on violent shows full of angry people. Somehow, we have come to believe that's the way life is.

As a young mom of two, when we went shopping I had expectations of how our kids should behave. When they didn't behave the way I wanted, I got angry, embarrassed, and upset. I threatened to punish them by not buying them anything. What a punishment! I didn't receive an instruction manual on how to raise kids. However, had I spent more time reading my Bible, I would have realized that was my instruction manual.

The Bible says that anger is always associated with foolishness, not wisdom. Take a look at these questions and answer them honestly.

Do you complain often?
Do you get upset when your expectations are not met?
Do you replay scenarios over and over in your head clouded by a negative perspective or just focus on your negative experiences?
Do you fume on the inside while wearing a fake smile?

Expressing negativity and complaining is often a sign that you have unresolved anger. Don't meditate on the negative scenarios in your life, meditate on the things above, the positive.

Perfectionism can cause you to become an angry person and bring much stress into your life as well as making those around you feel like they aren't good enough. Those who strive for perfection are driven by a constant need to perform and feel appreciated which makes it hard for them to truly rest. I will admit that I am a recovering perfectionist. Oftentimes we think we will be happy when everything is done right, and everyone is behaving the way we want but this pattern of thinking brings much frustration and anger. There was only one perfect person who walked this earth, His name was Jesus. Exchange your drive for perfection with His peace.

The Lord's Heart

Don't give in to anger, My child. Anger does not bring about the righteous life I have planned for you. Get your eyes off your own happiness and be more concerned with the happiness and welfare of others. Be a good witness for Me by demonstrating kindness, love, and grace to others. I've poured out My grace upon you, and in turn, you shall pour out that grace on others. Don't hold them to your standard or put expectations on how they are to behave, love them for who they are, and where they are now. Remember that your ways are not perfect, and neither are theirs.

I have given you all of the fruits of My Spirit, exercise the fruit of self-control over the thoughts that produce anger. This fruit will allow you to respond in wisdom, love, and in a spirit of gentleness. Ask Me to help you in exercising this fruit, I long to help you when you ask. Bring Me your unmet expectations, insults, hurts, etc. Together we will separate your emotions from the facts so you'll know the next step you need to take.

Forgiveness is the key that will unlock your happiness and set you free. Reconciliation and harmony is what I want for all My children. You are a wise person who keeps yourself under control, not under your strength and power, but Mine. You can do it, My child. Come quickly and talk to Me about your anger for I want you to go to bed in peace.

But the Lord answered and said to her, "Martha, Martha, you are worried and bothered about so many things; but only one thing is necessary, for Mary has chosen the good part, which shall not be taken away from her."
Luke 10:41-42

Declaration

I will walk in love and forgiveness toward all people.

Prayer

Abba Father, forgive me for my angry outbursts and selfish ways that aren't pleasing to You. Perfect me in Your love for others. Heal all past wounds and deliver me from anger and perfectionism. Holy Spirit, empower me to drop the expectations I place on people and just love them like You do. Lord, I don't want to be a complaining child forgetting to be grateful for all You have done for me. Give me a new heart of praise, worship, and contentment in all circumstances. In the name of Jesus, I forgive all those in generations, past and present, who lash out in anger or fear and I break that curse off my family line now. In Christ our Lord. Amen.

His Heart for Me

Do you get angry when your expectations are not met? How about when others don't treat you with respect or listen? Do you find yourself complaining about your circumstances or people? God wants to reveal the thought patterns and ways in which you interpret and react to certain situations, so you can understand why you are getting angry and be healed from it. He wants you to live a quiet and peaceful life. Get away with Him today.

Day 19

Relinquishing Control

Wait for the Lord; Be strong and let your heart take courage;
Yes, wait for the Lord.
Psalm 27:14

Thought for the Day: Trust God, He knows what He is doing.

The need to be in control has been a stronghold in my life. A strong tower that needed to be demolished. Around the age of fourteen, my mom and stepdad divorced and the only home I knew was ripped away from me. I went from living on a farm, doing chores, and riding horses to living in an apartment next to a bar with nothing to do. As an only child, the only one I could talk to was my mom, but she was busy with work and getting over the divorce. Mom and I were believers but far from Him. My life felt out of control. I was depressed, lonely, and scared. Everything I knew, my routine, my security, and comfort were gone. I started controlling what I ate so I could feel in control of something in my life. Eating a handful of grapes and a few crackers a day didn't provide enough nutrition. This lasted about six months before my mom threatened to take me to a center for anorexia.

When my husband and I had kids, I was called the control freak. Many things were off-limits because Mom was afraid for their safety. Unfortunately, I passed my fear along to them.

For many years I tried to manipulate God into answering my prayers more quickly. I did this by fasting and taking communion daily. Maybe this would make God move faster. Deny the flesh, and God will answer. My attempts were unsuccessful. All it did was cause frustration and doubt about God's goodness and timing in my life. I had the wrong heart motive. That had to change.

"Lord, I am tired and weary. I have been waiting and praying for breakthrough. I've tried fasting, praying more, taking communion daily. What will move Your hand? Fulfill Your word to me, Lord." Once I let go of my fears and my need to control everything, God's hand moved and I received my breakthrough. Let go and let God do a mighty work in you.

The Lord's Heart

I am the everlasting light. The days of your mourning shall be over. The work of My hands will comfort your heart. My love is everlasting and satisfies your lonely soul. I know you are waiting for breakthrough. You are praying faithfully and waiting for your prayers to be answered. The great I AM is faithful! You can trust Me. Receive your breakthrough in the midst of the waiting, fasting, and praying.

Don't give up, child. Don't lose hope in Me or My promises to you. I am fighting for you. I am pushing back the darkness with My light. I ride across the heavens to rescue you. Swiftly I come to help you in your time of need. My timing is perfect. Have patience in the waiting. All things will work out for your benefit and the benefit of others. My plans are better than your plans. My timing is better than yours, My child. Trust Me! I know what I am doing. Do you remember the times you jumped ahead of Me and My timing for you? My plans succeed! Relinquish your control. You are safe in My arms and My will.

For the vision is yet for the appointed time;
It hastens toward the goal and it will not fail.
Though it tarries, wait for it; For it will certainly come, it will not delay.
Habakkuk 2:3

Declaration

I will put my trust in the Lord and in His perfect timing.

Prayer

Abba Father, I ask that You purify my heart. Cause me to feel secure and confident in Your timing, while I trust in You for my breakthrough. Engrave on my heart that You know what You are doing, I don't need to have all the answers. Help me to be flexible about what You want to do in my life, not stubbornly holding onto my own plans. Strongholds of control be demolished now! Faith and trust in God, increase! Holy Spirit, highlight the areas in my life where I have wrongfully taken control so I can learn to release my control and let You lead fully. In Christ our Lord. Amen.

His Heart for Me

Are there areas in your life that you seem to be in control of that are off-limits to God? Who orders your steps? You or God? Are you in control of your finances? Do you find yourself manipulating others to try to control them? Seek the Lord concerning the things you need to take your hands off and give control to God.

Day 20

Passions and Idolatry

My people are destroyed for lack of knowledge.
Hosea 4:6

Thought for the Day: Overdosing on our passions can lead us into idolatry.

For over 30 years, I have fought and failed to have a healthy relationship with food. I've tried just about everything you can think of including diets, positive thinking, quoting scripture, starvation, rebuking the enemy, and cleaning up generational curses relating to food issues in my family line. Nothing seemed to last.

"Lord, I can't do this anymore. No amount of strength, positive thinking, or quoting Your truth is helping me to overcome this stronghold in my life. I need Your help in a big way. I need Your intervention and revelation. Is there something I have been missing? What is it, Lord?"

Out of the wind the Lord questioned me.

GOD: Pam, do you know that food has become an idol in your life? Every time you let your passions (strong emotions) or thoughts propel you towards food, you are committing idolatry.

PAM: What? Come again?

GOD: Why do you seek food for comfort? My Spirit is the greatest comforter you have been given. My Spirit gives you everlasting comfort without shame and guilt. Anytime you trust something or someone over Me, you commit idolatry. You put trust in food to make you feel better about yourself or the situation. Does that ever work? No, in fact, it always makes you feel shameful and guilty.

He then brought Colossians 3:5 to my awareness. *Put to death therefore what is earthly in you: sexual immorality, impurity, passion, evil desire, and covetousness, which is idolatry.*

The Lord had my attention. I sought forgiveness immediately. The conviction the Lord brings is easy to take if we are quick to repent. Once we repent, He is always faithful to forgive.

GOD: Pam, walk with Me.

The Spirit of the Lord led me into a thick part of our forest where He told me to pick some Yarrow. I picked seven stocks of Yarrow, breaking the roots off under my feet. The Lord encouraged me to pick one more and wrap it around the others in my hand. As I stood there holding my bouquet, I heard the Lord say:

"Not by might, but by My Spirit, you will overcome. All of satan's temptations are under your feet."

I realized that the Spirit of God had just led me through a prophetic act. It had a great impact on me in the spiritual and natural realm. "It is finished," I declared. I walked out of our forest a different woman. A woman equipped by His Spirit to overcome, a woman with a new understanding of idolatry, and a woman with a renewed mind and strengthened spirit.

Pause throughout the day and recognize your passions and the pressures you face. Recognize the thoughts that drive you, therein lies wisdom. Use your spiritual muscles to help you stop and think before reaching for unhealthy food. God will help us overcome every stronghold, if we ask for His help.

The Lord's Heart

Be diligent, dear child, and pay close attention to the desires and passions that drive you. Are they godly? Run to Me! I long to be the source of your happiness and joy. My joy is everlasting and does not fade. You can go through the motions of speaking scripture and praying but if your heart is not connected, there will be no freedom. Don't look at the behavior itself and seek a quick fix but ask Me for wisdom in discerning the root cause. Surrender all the passions within your heart to Me, the godly and ungodly. Be consumed with passion and hunger for Me.

Your emotions were created by Me. Many say you can't trust your feelings or emotions. However, they are an internal gauge alerting you to where you have placed your hope, what your heart loves, trusts, and fears. Let your emotions highlight the weak areas where your enemy will likely attack.

The great I AM is the source of everything good in your life. That quick happy fix you get from your endorphins rising is not true happiness or joy. It will always be short-lived. You will need to "do more" to increase your endorphins to stay in that "happy state." Child, this doesn't work. Some are exercising themselves crazily because they seek to be in that "fake" happy state continually. Exercising is good for you because it lowers stress and relieves pain by releasing endorphins but what will you do when the happy feelings go away? Will you run to the chocolate and the gym again or will you run to Me? Run to Me when you are stressed, and I will calm you with My presence.

But if any of you lacks wisdom, let him ask of God, who gives to all generously and without reproach, and it will be given to him.
James 1:5

Declaration

I will pursue God first before I do anything else to relieve my emotions.

Prayer

Abba Father, thank you for loving me and not finding fault with my lack of wisdom. I ask for more wisdom to overcome all temptations in my life. Mind of Christ increase, carnal mind decrease. Bring awareness to the thoughts that lead me astray. Holy Spirit, infuse me with Your power to stand firm in holy deeds and thoughts. Give me eyes to see like You did for Elisha's servant, enabling me to see what You are doing amid my trials, storms, and chaos. I declare that I will be attentive throughout my day, to the unseen holy realm around me. King of glory, have Your way in me and teach my heart to run after You. In Christ our Lord. Amen.

His Heart for Me

What do your passions, strong emotions, or thoughts drive you to do? Seek the Holy Spirit today. He will expose the ungodly passions and give you revelation. Your job is to repent for the things He shows you. In Greek, the word "repent" means to change one's mind for the better, to reconsider and think differently. The Holy Spirit's job is to empower you to overcome these things, so ask Him for the power. He has an unlimited supply.

Day 21

Think About What You Think About

Watch over your heart with all diligence,
for from it flow the springs of life.
Proverbs 4:23

Thought for the Day: Do my words edify and build up or do they tear down and cause stress?

One of the quickest ways to grieve God's spirit is through complaining and grumbling about our circumstances. It causes us to feel disconnected from Him. To get a handle on my complaining, I did some research by reading the Bible and a few other books about our words and how they bring life or death. During this time, I kept hearing this phrase, *Think about what you think about.*

This catchy little phrase caused me to do just that. During the day I wrote down my thoughts. At the end of the day I was completely shocked with how much negativity about myself and others was on my paper. Looking at all the dirt, mistakes, failures, and bad fruit in our lives and others will always make things seem worse than they are, heavier than they are, and cause hopelessness.

If we aren't careful, we can unknowingly release witchcraft out of our mouths by agreeing with the enemy instead of God. I need to believe what God says, not what the enemy or other people say about me. Often we need a makeover in our thought lives, a paradigm shift. We must resist looking at what's wrong and needs to be fixed and speak God's truth in faith. It will renew our minds.

The Lord prompted me to do a word fast for a month. These two books were my guides: *The Forty-Day Word Fast* by Tim Cameron and

Who Switched off My Brain? by Dr. Caroline Leaf. Our thoughts can be the source of our depression, anxiety, fear, and the diseases we suffer from today.

The word "fast" in the original Hebrew means to cover the mouth. Boy, did I need to do just that. While fasting from negative thoughts and words, I found myself speaking less and listening more. I was kinder to myself and others. It was really worth the time and effort.

At the end of this word fast, I noticed a significant change in my allergies. I had fewer skin reactions to wheat. I stopped breaking out in hives for no apparent reason. Cleaning chemicals stopped causing such horrendous headaches. When I got a handle on my thought life, 90% of my allergies went away. Praise be to God. The Holy Spirit will help direct us to God and keep our thoughts pure as we meditate on the truth. Keeping a handle on our thought life will be a lifelong adventure but all things are possible with God.

The Lord's Heart

Choose your words wisely, daughter/son of the Most High God. Extend forgiveness to those who irritate you. Look for the gold, for the truth of who I say they are. Look at how far people have come, how much you have changed, and the possibilities of further growth through intimacy with Christ. Live a lifestyle of celebrating others. My Spirit will equip you to live this way, just ask for help. Your body has a negative chemical reaction to every offense or criticism you don't release which affects your cells and causes headaches and tight necks. Those who hold to the belief that they have the right to be angry and hold on to their offenses, usually have stiff necks from the accumulated stress. Don't be stiff-necked and stubborn, actively resisting My Spirit instead be doers of the Word. When you have matured to the point that you are dead to self, you will give up all your rights to be offended and angry, and even the right to judge others. I will give much grace to the humble one who obeys My commands.

Release words that bring life to others. Meditate not on how others have wronged you but release My grace and mercy over them. Watch over your mouth with diligence, beloved. Bless and do not curse. Resist grumbling and complaining about your brothers and sisters, instead seek to bless, forgive, and intercede for them. Every time you choose to meditate on My words, you renew your mind. I love you, and I will empower you to overcome the battle of your thought life. Renew your mind daily with My words.

Finally, brethren, whatever is true, whatever is honorable, whatever is right, whatever is pure, whatever is lovely, whatever is of good repute, if there is any excellence and if anything worthy of praise, dwell on these things.
Philippians 4:8

Declaration

I will exchange my complaining for praising.

Prayer

Abba Father, increase the fruit of self-control in my life by Your Spirit. Help me to take captive those thoughts that don't line up with scripture and cast them down. Expose every lie I am believing about myself and others, and replace it with Your truth already written on my heart. Holy Spirit, I invite you into my life, and say, have Your way and rearrange my thoughts to mirror that of Jesus, my precious savior. Father, show me where I am agreeing with the devil instead of agreeing with You. I humbly admit my need for Your mighty and powerful hand helping me to gain control over my thought life. Help me, Jesus. In Christ our Lord. Amen.

His Heart for Me

What do you spend most of your time thinking about? Do you typically focus on how things went wrong in your day, how you were treated unkindly by your boss, etc. or are you thinking about Christ and the things above? Get with Jesus and evaluate your thought life today. None of us will be perfect in this, but we must seek to grow in maturity in our minds by renewing them with the Word of God constantly. Consider going through one of the books I recommended today.

COMMUNING
with GOD
My sheep hear My voice, and I know them,
and they follow Me.
John 10:27

His Tender Loving Care

For even the Son of Man did not come to be served, but to serve, and to give His life a ransom for many.
Mark 10:45

Thought for the Day: As a child of God who is seated in heavenly places, when I praise God I join heaven's choir in praising the Maker of the whole universe.

One morning as I happily strolled to our forested area, I wore a smile on my face. Love and joy filled my heart and I came expecting the Lord to show up and hang out with me. As I stepped into our forest, the wind picked up a little and blew through the beautiful Aspen trees. I then heard a voice in my spirit which I knew to be Jesus.

JESUS: Will you let Me wash your feet today, Pam?

PAM: Lord, You don't need to wash my feet. I want to honor You and wash Your feet. I want to kiss Your feet and pour out my affection on You. Will You manifest Yourself in the natural, so I can do this for You?

JESUS: You must hold still and let Me serve you and wash your feet, or you can have no part of Me.

I suddenly was brought into a vision of Jesus washing His disciples' feet but Peter did not want Jesus to wash his feet. Like Peter, why is it so hard for me to accept the Lord's love? Why is it so hard to allow Jesus to serve me in this way? It makes me very uncomfortable.

The Lord then set me in a vision where He washed my feet. I cried as He washed my feet, so tenderly and lovingly. Every fiber in my being wanted to get up and run away, but it was as if I was glued to my seat. As I sat, Jesus talked.

JESUS: Will you let Me take care of your basic needs? I love you, and wish to do good to you, and take care of you even as simply as cleaning your feet. There is intimacy and connection in serving others. I did not come to be served but to serve My Father's children on earth. To release the captives and set them free, and bring healing to the afflicted, this is why I came. Do you know that you bless Me with your words? You bless Me with your prayers and praise. Your worship and adoration towards Me pleases Me greatly.

PAM: I didn't know that, my Lord.

My face turned a nice shade of red and more tears flowed. His unconditional love has that effect on me.

JESUS: There is much rejoicing in heaven when your heart is engaged as you worship Me. Do you know that My Father has thousands of angels praising and worshipping Him? When you praise and celebrate Us, you are joining the heavenly choir.

PAM: Thank you for loving me with such an amazing, radical, unconditional love. I am honored that You would accept my praise, and that it pleases You and makes You smile. I don't feel worthy of Your love. Help me to accept it and embrace it more, O Lord.

The Lord's Heart

I AM the Lord Your God who takes care of all your needs. I will satisfy your soul and fill you with My love. I know My pure and undefiled love makes you uncomfortable. You run from Me because you think you are not deserving of My love. I will teach you to enjoy it and accept it with open arms and feet firmly planted. How could I not love you? You are My child. My love is a gift to you. You can't earn it, it is free. Accept it and soak it up, My child, into the very depths of your soul. Let My abundant love flow through you. In time, it will transform the way you think about Me and love Me. You are only accepting a fraction of My love right now, but there is so much more available to you. My love is abundant, it never runs dry. It is like the ocean waves, constant and everlasting. With every wave of love, I will refresh your entire being. You are My child, a citizen of My Kingdom, in heaven and on earth forevermore.

And suddenly there appeared with the angel a multitude of the heavenly host praising God and saying, "Glory to God in the highest, And on earth peace among men with whom He is pleased."
Luke 2:13-14

Declaration

I will sit and let Him wash my feet today.

Prayer

Abba Father, thank you for Your abundant love. Teach me to hold still and accept Your love in every part of my heart, mind, and soul. I am deciding in advance to not run from You when You show up. For me to survive life on earth, I must be filled completely with Your love. When I understand how much I am loved and adored, then I will love myself in healthy ways and also my neighbor as I love myself. Lord, help me make the time to let You wash my feet today. Holy Spirit, fill my vision with a picture of Jesus.
In Christ our Lord. Amen.

His Heart for Me

Do you willingly accept His love for you or do you tend to run from intimacy? Did you get hurt from letting your guard down once? You can be completely transparent, close and real with the Lord. He will not hurt you. Trust Him, He is trustworthy. Imagine Jesus washing your feet. Listen for what He will speak to you and record your intimate encounter here. Intimacy simply means this: Someone you are closely acquainted with and devoted to.

Day 23

Cling To Me

You shall follow the LORD your God and fear Him; and you shall keep His commandments, listen to His voice, serve Him, and cling to Him.
Deuteronomy 13:4

Thought for the Day: Pursuing God is not a works thing, it is a pursuit of resting in His love and presence.

PAM: Good morning, Lord.

GOD: Cling to Me!

PAM: What does that even mean, Lord?

GOD: Pam, I want you to cling to Me like you would cling to water if you had gone without it for three days.

PAM: Wow, that is really desperate, Lord.

I felt guilty for not pursuing God like this all the time. When I'm in a storm, I pursue Him like this but not when everything is going okay.

GOD: Pam, don't feel shame and guilt, that is not from Me.

PAM: Okay, Lord. I need more understanding if I am not going to feel that way.

GOD: Do you remember when you first fell in love? How your entire being was overwhelmed with this person? You would think about them all day, your future, your entire vision was filled with them. In fact, walls could have been crumbling down around you and you wouldn't have noticed. This is the kind of love pursuit I desire from you.

My heart understood. My whole vision is to be saturated with the Lord, to spend time in His presence. In Hebrew, the word for cling is "dabaq." Other meanings are: closely pursued, stick together, held fast, and stuck.

As we dig into the Bible, we find the importance of clinging to God. In Numbers 13-14, we see Caleb and Joshua clinging to God's promises. They saw the same things the other ten spies saw. The difference was these two men rested in the fact that God had promised them this land and so the giants would be defeated. Nothing was impossible for the Lord. Not only did they decide to cling to the promise of possessing the land as an everlasting inheritance but that all the promises of the great I AM were true.

Take time to cling to the Lord and His promises. Find ten minutes in your day and sit quietly with the Lord. Don't overload Jesus with your needs. Come with no need, just the desire to be in His presence. And in return, He will overwhelm your entire being with His love.

The Lord's Heart

Forget not all that I have done for you. Forget not every answered prayer. Forget not the sacrifice of My precious Son. Remember to not look at the giants and impossible situations before you. I long for you to think higher, trust higher, and to look up. You have an army of angels ready to help you. You have the power of the Holy Spirit to speak My decrees and promises over your life and the lives of those you love. Don't listen to the naysayers and doubting people among you. Put your trust in Me and what I can do through you.

Clinging to Me is the same as loving Me. When you cling to Me, you are showing Me that you are putting your trust in My abilities instead of your own. I have promised to fight for you. In the time period of Joshua, one of his men put to flight a thousand for I was fighting for them as they continued to cling to Me. You are to cling to Me in the same fashion. It doesn't matter how many are against you when you have Me with you. You could be standing on a battlefield with ten thousand against you and they would all fall as you go forward because I am fighting on your behalf. Jesus is with you and they shall all run away. There shall not be one left standing when you know that We are with you. Doubt not My goodness towards you.

But you are to cling to the Lord your God, as you have done to this day.
Joshua 23:8

Declaration

I shall cling to the Lord with all my heart, soul, and mind.

Prayer

Abba Father, I will seek to cling to You in all circumstances. You shall be my first love, always. Thank you for giving me the mind of Christ. May my mind be overflowing with thoughts of You and Your goodness. I declare that I will take time to listen and hang out with You. Lord, forgive me if I have doubted Your Word or promises to me in any way. Holy Spirit, increase my faith in God. I shall look past the chaos around me and find my precious savior standing in my midst. In Christ our Lord. Amen.

His Heart for Me

Do you cling to God in times of stress or do you cling to something or someone else? Joshua warned the Israelites before he died not to go back to loving and clinging to the nations that remained among them. If they turned back to trusting in the nations among them, they would be a thorn, snare, and trap to the Israelites. Ask Jesus if you have been clinging to anything other than Him and record it here.

Day 24

Unmasking the Real

Your eyes are too pure to approve evil, And You can not look on wickedness with favor. Why do You look with favor on those who deal treacherously? Why are You silent when the wicked swallow up those more righteous than they?
Habakkuk 1:13

Thought for the Day: I can be real with God.

Often we use other things to mask the unforgiveness and bitterness in our hearts. Personally, I tried covering up my troubles by putting on a mask of happiness. I'd eat sugar to help relieve the pain, but that happiness was only temporary. There was so much pain in my life that had been stuffed down since I was a young teenager. At one point I sat down to write letters to those I needed to forgive as a means of releasing some of my pain. What happened surprised me. As I wrote, I broke pencils from pressing so hard on the paper. I threw pencils and tore into the paper as I was writing. The nice, quiet, shy Christian woman who was holding it all together, exploded. There was a volcano of anger inside of me.

The pages were filled with foul language. I don't use foul language, but there was a lot of foul, soul language on those pages. All the poison of unforgiveness and bitterness was released. I felt amazingly free as I threw those letters in the fireplace. The hard work of being real about my pain and extending forgiveness to others was completed. A hint of shame remained and I felt embarrassed before God but an enormous amount of pain was released.

A few years went by. Overall I was doing better at loving others and was feeling pretty happy. The Lord impressed upon me that I wasn't finished yet. I had two more to forgive. Who was on the list? God and myself. I decided I better forgive God first. God was revealing to me all the things I blamed Him for. Here are a few questions I had for Him:

Why did You take the only good earthly father I had?
Why did You allow my stepfather to speak lies into my life?
Why didn't You bring me another good, godly father who would love me right?
Where were You when I tried taking my life?
Why didn't You stop the abuse?
Why didn't You stop the miscarriage?
WHERE WERE YOU????

I approached Him in respect and reverence, knowing that it sounded quite silly that "God needed to be forgiven." He didn't need to be forgiven. I wrestled with this for quite a while. I had Christians rebuke me for even saying that I needed to forgive God. "God doesn't ever need to be forgiven" was their response. "Yes, I know that, BUT, my heart is screaming at Him" was always my reply. I decided to ignore those Christians and get REAL with God. I yelled, I screamed, I cried, I asked Him to forgive me for being mad at Him. At some point He said,

"I can take it, let it out!"

I continued… I felt guilty for yelling at Him, but He never once condemned me for it. Never once gave up on me or got angry with me.

He just kept saying, **"Let it out, I am a big boy!"**

I fell in a heap, it was not pretty. God intervened as I lay on the floor in a pool of tears. My heavenly Father wrapped His loving arms around me. This was the first time I felt God's tangible love for me. God showed me how He was working in my life. That day I walked away free of my burdens. I felt light like a feather. I didn't realize how much He loved me until I let my anger out. I was hiding and pretending everything was fine and thought, "Good Christians don't get mad at God." I'm not saying it is good to be angry with God, not at all! However, if you find that you are, let it out and talk to God about it! He can take it! In fact, He wants you to release it to Him.

When we find ourselves mad at God, it's because we have such little understanding about His love for us and His goodness towards us.

Don't use a mask of religiosity to hide your anger. God and I had a conversation about the error of my thinking.

GOD: Pam, I was there when you tried to take your life. You are still here, aren't you? I rescued you six times. I always sent someone to stop you, don't you remember?

PAM: Yes, I can see that now, Lord.

GOD: Pam, I did stop the abuse. I sent someone to you, so you could move out. Remember?

PAM: Yes, Lord, I remember.

I still couldn't understand the death of my father and the miscarriage but I no longer needed answers, I had peace. For every accusation and lie, He showed me the truth or simply gave me peace. God walked me through the scene again, showing me where He was and what He was doing. In the end, I thanked God for His goodness and praised Him for His intervention throughout my younger years. I learned that God is always good even when we suffer the consequences of someone else's sin. My trust in God grew exponentially.

There are many people in the Bible that were real with God including Habakkuk, David, and Job. Job does not restrain his mouth from complaining and asking God questions. Basically, Job complains for thirty-seven chapters. God's reply to Job was this, "Will the faultfinder contend with the Almighty? Let him who reproves God answer it." (Job 40:2) This is a pretty serious response from God. Job responds by putting his hand on his mouth and repents in dust and ashes.

We need to be real with God and talk to Him about what is on our mind and the burdens of our heart. However, we must be ready for His reply and repent when He shows us the error of our thinking.

The Lord's Heart

From now on, I want you to always be real with Me. I can handle all of your emotions. If you are mad at Me because you feel like I have let you down or didn't answer one of your prayers, come to Me and talk with Me about it. The hurt you feel will only fester and put up a wall between us if you don't share it. I will give you the truth. I will reveal My will and mysteries to you if you are open to My ways. Remember, My ways are higher than your ways and My thoughts are higher than your thoughts. I will slice through the turmoil and reveal the heart of the matter.

Pam, let's say that there are two young boys wanting to trade baseball cards. One has a worn out, ripped up Babe Ruth card and the other boy has a gold-plated, never touched Babe Ruth card. The boy with the worn and ripped baseball card represents your ways, thoughts, and understanding concerning the things that happened in your life. All you see are the tears and dirt of your life. The gold-plated card represents My ways and will for your life. You need My perspective—love. There are many things that happened to you that were not part of My will for your life however I helped you through them all. I had a plan for saving you from yourself and others.

Some things you suffered by the hands of others because they used their free will for evil and other things you have suffered were the result of exercising your own free will. Child, I will turn all things to good as you forgive others and yourself. You may not understand everything you had to go through, or will go through, but My promise to you is that I will help you through it and turn it to good. Will you hand Me your worn-out tattered card called "your will and understanding" for My gold-plated will for your life? The word "forgiveness" is stamped on the front of My card. Make the trade, dearly beloved. The death of My Son allows you to keep My gold-plated card for eternity if you will only let go of your own worn-out card.

Come to Me, all who are weary and heavy-laden, and I will give you rest. Take My yoke upon you and learn from Me, for I am gentle and humble in heart, and You Will Find Rest For Your Souls. For My yoke is easy and My burden is light.
Matthew 11:28-30

Declaration

I will always be real with God,
knowing that He can handle all of my emotions.

Prayer

Abba Father, help me to shed the masks that protect me from letting others know how I really feel. Teach me how to speak to others in love while sharing how I feel even if it is different from how they feel. Lord, fill my mouth with Your words and make me an effective communicator. Thank you for welcoming all my questions when I see things not lining up to scripture. Holy Spirit, assist me in speaking truth. May I learn to not hide anything from You for You know all things. Lord, keep me from being a faultfinder, like you did for Job. I love you, Elohim, and I thank you.

In Christ our Lord. Amen.

His Heart for Me

Are you unknowingly mad at God? Do you have bitterness against Him because He didn't answer one of your prayers the way you wanted? Do you find yourself finding fault with God or others? Quiet yourself down, turn on some soaking music, music without words and ask the Holy Spirit to expose anything that you might be holding against God. Beloved, let no wall separate us. Be honest and real with Me, says the Lord.

Day 25

Healed in His Presence

You will make known to me the path of life; In Your presence is fullness of joy; In Your right hand there are pleasures forever.
Psalm 16:11

Thought for the Day: When we put our problems and hurts in God's hands, He puts His love and peace in our hearts.

Broken and saved individuals can be the best ministers to those who are lost in our world. Why? Because we can relate to their problems. Those who don't understand brokenness have a harder time relating to others who are broken. We all have brokenness, whether we admit it or not.

The biggest concern is what our brokenness can pour out onto others. Does our brokenness contain bitterness, anger, or a negative mindset? If yes, then we need to go to Jesus and repent for what isn't pleasing to Him before ministering to others. Do a heart check before you open your mouth and pray for others, whether ministering on the streets or at church.

Our wounds and the pain we have experienced, God will use to bring release to another. The Lord doesn't want us to stay broken. He wants us to be healed from it all and live lives full of peace, joy, and freedom. Our testimonies can be the breakthrough others need. When we share our testimonies of how God got us through our trials, we bring healing to others and invite them to be free as well. Get comfortable sharing your story.

One morning God spoke to me about my brokenness.

GOD: How do you see your life, Pam?

PAM: I see my life as a broken jar surrounded by shattered pieces. I'm still missing pieces that were stolen by others.

GOD: Will you let Me mend your broken heart and put back all those pieces with My presence? Will you hold still and accept My love? My love is perfect. I know that My love makes you uncomfortable and causes you to run and squirm. Please sit with Me and hold still. My presence is like liquid gold. It will run through your entire being gathering all the broken pieces and filling in the places you believe are lost. My pure gold from heaven is sticky like glue. It will hold you together perfectly. As you sit still and lean back against My chest, I will heal you. I will transform and heal all those broken places with the power of My presence. The jar you see is not the jar I see. The jar I see is captivating, it intrigues Me. I will give you the ability to see through My eyes, so you may see how breathtaking your appearance is to Me. My compassion for you is endless.

PAM: There is nothing better than spending time with You, Lord. I will hold still and soak up all Your love for me. I will restrain myself from running, knowing that Your love won't hurt me. Thank you for embracing me and overlooking all my faults. Thank you for loving me perfectly without conditions. Wave after wave of Your love crashes over me, I am completely satisfied. Your love enables me to face the day. You are a gracious God and I adore You. You are overwhelmingly good to Your children.

The Lord's Heart

Climb up into My lap and rest your head on My chest for a while, My child. My love is pure and will flow through you like honey and gold. My love will mend all the broken places of your heart. This is My requirement for you: That you forgive others and confess your sins to Me, dear child. Remember not to play the blame game but step back and ask Me for revelation concerning the heartbreak you are experiencing. Let go of all bitterness and resentment so I can place My heavenly healing balm on your wounded heart. I will strengthen you to carry on. Just surrender to Me. New people will arrive to help you walk through this time in your life. Don't despise your struggles, for maturity will come from this. I will replenish your joy and happiness. Refrain from complaining, it will not help you. As I pour My tangible love over you, contentment and peace will fill your soul, even in the chaos.

He heals the brokenhearted and binds up their wounds.
Psalm 147:3

Declaration

God has healed my broken heart.

Prayer

Abba Father, You are so gracious to me. Thank you for healing my broken heart. Your love makes me melt. Your tangible love cleanses my heart. I melt in the peace of Your presence. As I release all my hurts to You, I shall experience the fullness of Your joy. Holy Spirit, bring back everything that was wrongfully stolen from me by my enemy. Everything the locust ate and stole from me; come back, now! I ask for a ten-fold return. Praise and honor to God Almighty! In Christ our Lord. Amen.

His Heart for Me

What did the locust steal from you? What does your enemy steal from you every day? Does your heart need healing? Have you opened a door to the devil through unforgiveness due to trauma or abuse? I know it is hard to forgive those who hurt you but you have been commanded by Jesus, to forgive others. Write down that which has been stolen from you and call it back with interest. Take time to rest your head on Jesus' chest today and receive His healing touch.

Day 26

No Longer a Sinner

No one who is born of God practices sin, because His seed abides in him; and he cannot sin, because he is born of God.
1 John 3:9

Thought for the Day: I am no longer a slave to sin but a saint and slave to righteousness.

PAM: Why do bad things happen to good people?

GOD: Pam, define good people to Me.

PAM: You're right, Lord. We are all sinners and fall short of Your glory.

GOD: Pam, you compare sins. Thinking that some are worse than others. Sin is sin. You were in the same boat with murderers headed to hell before you accepted Me. I drew you to Me and you are not called a sinner anymore but a saint. You are now a slave to righteousness instead of sin. Now you are dead to sin.

PAM: Thank you, Lord. Help me to understand more.

GOD: Pam, I give My children free will to make decisions. I don't want to rule over My people with an iron fist. Many make bad decisions and suffer the consequences and bring suffering upon others, even believers are not exempt from these consequences. How do I help My people live a life pleasing to Me? I have put My laws in their minds and written them on their hearts. Jesus, My good and perfect Son, came to earth to wash away repented sins. My people have the mind of Christ and My Spirit to help them along the way. They have the tools to live an abundant life, but many are rebellious and turn away from My help and love. What are the consequences of someone who chooses to fill their body with junk food and sugar?

PAM: They will gain weight, not have the proper vitamins, and are more susceptible to diabetes or cancer.

GOD: That is correct. My people are destroyed by their lack of knowledge. Many decisions are made from ignorance, not sin. Many blame Me wrongly. The devil has laid out many snares. I love My people and want nothing but the best for them. I want all to live abundant, fruitful lives, full of peace and joy. That is why I have given them free access to Me and My Spirit. Remember this: Once you believe in Jesus and repent, I no longer call you a sinner but a saint, and child of My Kingdom. Don't call yourself a sinner anymore because that life passed away, dear child. You might sin here and there but that does not make you a sinner. Your life was purchased by My Son's blood. You were welcomed into My family on the day of your baptism. Sinners don't live in heaven. Saints live in heaven. I have given you permission to call yourself a saint. I am calling you to view yourself from My heavenly perspective, beloved saint. Start calling yourself a saint.

PAM: Thank you, Lord, for being so good to us. I praise you for calling me to righteousness. Thank you for calling me a saint instead of still calling me a sinner even when I sin and mess up.

GOD: Everything you suffer while on earth whether that be from nature, in body, from others, from godly decisions or poor decisions, will be turned for your good. You might not recognize or see the good but when you stand before Me I will make all things clear and known.

The Lord's Heart

Your past sins have been washed away, don't meditate on them or feel bad about them any longer, dear child. The only time it is beneficial for you to look back at your past sins is when you are helping another child of mine get free from sin. Share where you once were and how I have delivered you through My love and forgiveness. This will bring hope and encouragement to others. Their faith will rise to believe that they too can be delivered and set free.

You have been created in My image, dear child. I gave you the gift of free will. Aren't you glad you have the freedom to make your own decisions? I want you to choose to obey Me and love Me on your own.

If I stripped you of this gift and made you obey Me, that would be love through manipulation, not pure and undefiled love. With great patience, I wait for My children to choose to love and obey Me. My commandments are written on your heart; now it is up to you to choose rightly. Every time you choose Me, I rejoice. When you follow the leading of My Spirit, and not your flesh, I smile upon you. From My throne in heaven, I celebrate your obedience. Remember that I love you through everything. My eyes are not filled with disappointment when you fail. My hand is forever stretched towards you, longing to pull you close to My heart for a warm and loving embrace.

Or do you not know that all of us who have been baptized into Christ Jesus have been baptized into His death? Therefore we have been buried with Him through baptism into death, so that as Christ was raised from the dead through the glory of the Father, so we too might walk in newness of life. For if we have become united with Him in the likeness of His death, certainly we shall also be in the likeness of His resurrection, knowing this, that our old self was crucified with Him, in order that our body of sin might be done away with, so that we would no longer be slaves to sin; for he who has died is freed from sin.

Romans 6:3-7

Declaration

I am a saint.

Prayer

Abba Father, thank you for rescuing me from a life of sin. Thank you for calling me a saint even though I will occasionally sin. May I continually grow in the likeness of Christ all the days of my life. Father, thank you for not ruling over me with an iron fist. I am grateful You are not like that, Daddy. Thank you for the gift of free will and the empowerment of the Holy Spirit to choose righteously. Holy Spirit, I am grateful for Your indwelling power, assist me in using this power well. Increase all of Your fruits in my life. In Christ our Lord. Amen.

His Heart for Me

Do you view yourself as a sinner or a saint? Remember that your old nature has been crucified with Christ. Are there any areas in your life where you would like to make better choices? Believe what the Word says, you have all the power you need to overcome every temptation. You have all the power you need to make the best choice. Spend some time with our glorious King seeking His heart.

Day 27

Cultivating True Humility

For everyone who exalts himself will be humbled,
and he who humbles himself will be exalted.
Luke 14:11

Thought for the Day: Humility is not thinking less of yourself, it is thinking of yourself less. —C. S. Lewis

---

When we are constantly cutting ourselves down, we aren't loving who God created us to be. Throughout the Body of Christ, I have often heard these comments: He must increase, I must decrease; it wasn't me, it was the Lord; I need to crucify my flesh; I am too humble to say that or be used by the Lord in that manner, and I am just a worm. These statements may contain some truth, but may also keep us trapped in insecurity and false humility. We are called to walk in the power of the Holy Spirit. If we are so focused on crucifying ourselves and beating ourselves up, will we ever rise to fulfill the calling He has on our lives? Friends, this is false humility at its sneakiest. You are talking the religious talk of humility but walking in pride.

When we reject compliments and cut ourselves down, we are taking a hammer to our identity in Christ. Being insecure will not keep you humble. For many years I rejected compliments as a means of keeping my pride in check. I never considered that it was Christ in me that was shining brightly through my love and actions causing people to give praise in the first place. People were actually complimenting the Jesus in me, which brought much glory to God. The same is true for you.

Humble people aren't absorbed with themselves but have listening ears and their eyes are focused on others. True humility says, "Jesus used me to heal so and so. Isn't God amazing?" Humble people can laugh at themselves when they make mistakes without damaging the royal priests they are. Friends, God made us to share in His glory.

What can we do to cultivate true humility? Keeping with repentance, being open to receiving correction, forgiving and speaking well of others, being willing to be last, serving others, and socializing with the homeless will keep our hearts humble.

Knowing that you can do nothing without God is a blessing. When this is your truth, you will walk in greater humility. Staying humble will be a lifelong pursuit. Don't feel bad about where you are, seek to find your full confidence in Him.

PAM: Lord, with every gift You give or increase in anointing, I feel the need to ask You to "keep me humble." Pride starts to rise up along with an attitude of "I am better than others." I dislike these thoughts and feelings. I say, "No" to that kind of thinking. Lord, keep me humble at all costs, but maybe without the thorn? That would be great. Alright, alright, do what You need to do. I surrender.

This was a scary prayer, "Keep me humble at all costs." The Lord answered this prayer. For several weeks, I was keenly aware of all the pride within me. Daily I repented as my pride was poked by others. This was not punishment, as some would believe, but a plan to bring awareness to areas in my life that needed cleansing. Scripture says that pride comes before destruction and I wanted to avoid that at all costs.

GOD: Do you think cutting yourself down in front of others makes you humble? You are feeding insecurity, not humility. Love yourself, love who I have made you to be. As I work through you, I, the Lord, will be glorified. Accept encouragement and compliments from others by simply saying, "Thank you." I will make you humble without needing to reject compliments, hate yourself, or beat yourself up.

When someone points out an error or fault, be humble enough to say, "Thank you for telling me, I'll go talk with the Lord concerning this matter." It is okay to laugh at yourself when you make a mistake. I know you're not perfect, so don't expect that of yourself. Don't reject negative or hurtful things said about you right away. There might be something I want you to recognize. Bring it to Me and ask if there is any truth in it. Apologize and admit your errors but don't meditate on your faults.

David took down Goliath because David had confidence in what I could do through him. He had faith in Me, not himself. His brother Eliab accused him of being prideful and full of deceit. It wasn't David who was full of pride and deceit, it was Eliab. When you walk in confidence and security of who I made you to be and what I can do through you, it may look like pride to others. When David came boasting about what I could do through him, it made his brother uncomfortable and exposed his lack of confidence in Me and his own insecurity. Your confidence must rest in Me. Rejoice in what I do through you. Remember, that anything is possible for the one that believes.

The Lord's Heart

Humility will be seen in My children when they follow Me. It is a character trait tied around your waist, always present, always buckled. Jesus humbly followed My plan for His life, you are to do the same, beloved. Come humbly before Me and I will lift you up in due time. Clothe yourself with compassion, kindness, humility, gentleness, and patience. Be completely patient, bearing with one another in love. You will receive great abundance and favor as you walk in humility. Mary, the mother of Jesus, was humble which is why I choose her to carry My Son. Her humility is what opened the doors of favor in heaven. Praying is a good way to humble yourself before Me for you are acknowledging your need for My help and insight. Those who humble themselves shall be exalted.

When you remain humble, you will grow in wisdom for you will listen to My instructions and the advice of those around you. Every time you feel pride start to rise within you, cast down those thoughts and vain imaginations. Refocus your eyes on Me instead of yourself. I will keep you humble if you are willing to pray and ask Me to keep you humble. Don't be afraid to pray that scary prayer. I will equip you to cast down pride and overcome it with great humility through the mind of Christ. Be willing to let Me show you where pride is hiding in your life. All of My children must learn to deal with the pride that rises up against the ways of My Spirit.

When pride comes, then comes dishonor,
But with the humble is wisdom.
Proverbs 11:2

Declaration

I will concern myself with what is right; not who is right.

Prayer

Abba Father, I surrender to You and ask that Holy Spirit have His way in my life. Reveal any false humility that has been hiding in my life. Root out all pride for I don't want destruction to come upon me. Holy Spirit, remind me to keep with repentance all the days of my life. Help me to accept compliments but not think too highly of myself. I declare that I will rejoice in what You are doing through me as You and I work together to accomplish Your will on earth to expand Your Kingdom. Thank you for choosing to work through me. It is an honor to do Your will on earth.

In Christ our Lord. Amen.

His Heart for Me

Are you brave enough to pray and ask God to keep you humble at all costs? You might get poked. Are you ready for God to reveal where pride is hiding in your life? Don't avoid the sting of pride being revealed but let Him root it out. God has many ways to reveal our pride so be open to what He highlights. God understands and doesn't condemn us for our pride. He will empower you to let go of it and walk in great humility. Record your brave prayer here.

Day 28

Joyful Adventures with Jesus

A joyful heart makes a cheerful face,
But when the heart is sad, the spirit is broken.
Proverbs 15:13

Thought for the Day: The Lord likes to have fun and laugh.

PAM: Good morning, Lord. This morning, I praise You for who You are. You answer as quickly as I think a question. How I adore You! You are so gracious to us. What would You like me to do today, Lord? Read scripture, pray for someone specific, worship? What's on the agenda?

JESUS: Pam, let's go have fun in a vision this morning.

PAM: Okay. Where? What? My mouth immediately closed, as I waited for His response.

The next thing I knew I was on the beach standing in front of Jesus. I was about nine years old and we were both barefoot. The sleeves of His robe hung several inches below His arms. I shoved both my arms up His arm sleeves and giggled loudly. Joyous laughter filled the air. His hearty deep laugh echoed across the beach touching the very depths of my being.

"I can be goofy and fun with the Lord?" I questioned myself.

Suddenly He turned and ran down the beach, beckoning me to chase after Him. As I started running, I realized I was now a teenager. To my surprise, He was still laughing and loving me. I thought to myself, "You still want to have fun with me even though I am a disobedient teenager?" This thought quickly faded as I soaked in His love for me.

We continued having fun as we sat on the sand, rolled down the beach, and enjoyed the beauty of the day. Suddenly a white horse galloped up to us and stopped, waiting patiently.

JESUS: Let's ride.

PAM: Where are the saddle and bridle?

JESUS: We don't need them, He said with a twinkle in His eye.

Jesus jumped up on the beautiful horse and reached for me, swinging me up on the back of the horse like I was a feather. Off we galloped down the beach. I couldn't stop laughing. The horse knew exactly where to go, when to stop, etc. Jesus spoke to the horse, spirit to spirit with no audible words. I was in awe of everything. The horse turned quickly and galloped out into the water, and then began swimming. Suddenly his legs stopped kicking, and we were all floating. Jesus and I just sat on the horse like surfers sitting on their surfboards waiting for a wave. We talked as we waited. I wasn't sure why we were waiting.

Next a dolphin appeared, and the horse disappeared. Jesus and I went gliding through the water with the dolphin. As quickly as I was brought into this vision, I left the vision. For several minutes I sat on the couch awestruck at all the fun I had with Jesus. I could have stayed all day with Him there.

PAM: Wow, that was fun, Lord! I didn't know You were so much fun or so funny. You really like to have fun with us, don't You?

JESUS: Yes, I love to have fun. I have a humorous side. I'm not as serious as you think I am. I want you to lighten up, Pam, and have more fun.

PAM: I can see that now. Yes, I want to lighten up and have more fun every day of my life.

Since this vision, I always have a smile on my face and joy in my heart. I often delight in His sense of humor and remember our fun times together.

The Lord's Heart

Beloved, many people believe I am angry with them, looking for ways to punish them. This is not true. My heart's desire is to show them My love and bless them. For those who don't know Me, I will allow certain things to happen that will draw them to Me. There are numerous chances for My people to repent and accept Me. Some have to hit rock bottom before they will accept Me. It hurts My heart to see them turn away again and again. Oh, how I long for all to be saved!

I want to reveal My humorous and fun side to all My children. Each child of mine has fun in different ways. For some, it will be dancing, singing, and laughing, and for others, it might look differently. However, laughter is good medicine for all My children. I long to see you in heaven with Us, beloved. The wedding feast shall be a grand party with lots of laughter and joyous melodies from the hearts of My children. All who believe in Christ are welcome to the party of a lifetime in heaven. Until we meet again…

He will yet fill your mouth with laughter
And your lips with shouting.
Job 8:21

Declaration

The Lord wants to have fun with me.

Prayer

Abba Father, forgive me for thinking You are boring and angry. Holy Spirit, continue to reveal to me how wonderful Jesus is. Open my eyes to His fun-loving and humorous side. Lord, thank you for wanting to have adventures with all Your children. Show me the height and depth of Your love through visions. Let me feel the warmth of Your love on my skin today. I long to have fun with You all the days of my life. Where shall we go, Lord? I am ready to go on many adventures with You.

In Christ our Lord. Amen.

His Heart for Me

Record your fun day with the Lord here. The places and things you enjoy are usually the places He wants to take you. Go have some fun with the Lord and be open to His plans. Simply ask, Lord, where do you want to take me today? Then patiently wait. Be aware of all your senses. Rest and look for the images He will place before your eyes. Having fun with Jesus can be a lifelong adventure.

EMBRACING JESUS
Our First Love
So now faith, hope, love abide, these three;
but the greatest of these is love.
1 Corinthians 13:13

The Prince of Peace

And who of you by being worried can add a single hour to his life?
Matthew 6:27

Thought for the Day: Give Jesus a gift bag full of all your worries and concerns. He will unwrap each worry, take note of it, then place the burden back in the bag and toss the whole thing behind His back declaring, "It is finished!" Hallelujah!

Why do I worry so much? I worry that I am not teaching my home-schooled children well. Worrying about their future and mine keeps me awake at night. Cancer runs in my family - will I get cancer too? Overwhelming thoughts about the things I seemingly have no control over flood my mind. Worrying doesn't add anything to my life except frazzled nerves.

When I stop meditating on my worries and take them to the Lord, peace saturates my entire being. My heart stops racing. His perspective becomes my perspective. Deleting the words "what if" from my vocabulary helps me loosen my clenched fists and put my unwarranted fears in God's hands in exchange for His peace. Prayer makes me feel like "Daddy" is in control and I can trust Him to work out all the things that worry me.

During one of my frazzled worried times, my chest tightened, and my heart raced. I did the only thing I knew to do. I looked up to the Lord for help, strength, and insight, and He spoke…

The Lord's Heart

Dearly beloved, why are you worried today? I am still with you. I haven't left your side. Are you worried about the future? Are you worried about your job or a friend who is sick? Give Me all your worries. Worrying doesn't add a single thing to your life. In fact, it just makes you tired and weary and causes you to age far too quickly. Abandon your internal negative dialogue and meditate on the Prince of Peace. I will calm you as you look to Me.

Do you see how I feed the robins? They don't store food. Do you see how I clothe the fields with wildflowers? I cause the rains to come and give them drink. I want to give you a refreshing drink of My Spirit. Drink up, dearly beloved.

I long to carry your burdens for you. I am the one who can do something about them. Ask for help and you shall receive. Be willing to let go of your concerns, control, and preconceived ideas about what needs to happen. You must lay your worries and burdens down at the cross and walk away empty-handed. Do not return to the cross to pick up your burdens and be yoked in bondage again. Throw off the chains of worry that bind you. I have given you the mind of Christ so you have the ability to think like Us. Rest, My child, and trust Me, knowing that I will work all things out for your good. Release, Release, Release them to Me. The great I AM is the only one qualified to carry your burdens and the only one who can do something about them.

Cease striving and know that I am God.
Psalm 46:10

Declaration

I will trust in God's plans for my life and my family's life.

Prayer

Abba Father, I am rolling up my sleeves and diving into prayer so I can be light and free from all yokes of slavery. Empower me to unload all unnecessary burdens and drop them at Your feet, Jesus. I pray my trust in You increases. Make me content with Your perfect timing, Father. Holy Spirit, increase the fruit of patience in my life while I wait for God to answer my prayers. Prince of Peace, help me to manage and process my stress so it won't affect my body negatively. For You have good plans for me, plans to prosper me and not harm me. In Christ our Lord. Amen.

His Heart for Me

What do you typically worry about? Some worries can be eliminated by making some much needed changes. Others we have no control over and must be released to the Lord. Make a list of your worries and concerns, then present them to the Lord and ask Him what your responsibility is for each one, if any. Then watch Christ toss those worries over His back and hear Him say, "I've got a plan for each concern."

Day 30

Loving Others More Than Yourself

Be of the same mind toward one another;
do not be haughty in mind, but associate with the lowly.
Do not be wise in your own estimation.
Romans 12:16

Thought for the Day: View others better than yourself.

Loving ourselves is often easier than loving others. I used to have a bad habit of ignoring others who were different than me. Several years ago at a women's retreat, I noticed a girl in a wheelchair who was physically and mentally challenged. During worship, many of the women were dancing around waving flags and clapping their hands. One of the speakers wheeled the girl in the wheelchair to the front so she could be included. Leaning over, she said, "Jesus is dancing with you." The girl smiled.

The leader then called for a circle dance. At least twenty women began singing and dancing around the young girl. Joyous laughter bounced off the walls. Time stood still as she danced with Jesus by twirling around in her chair. The radiance of her smile lit up the room. No one cared who was getting the attention. No one was fighting to be in the spotlight. The manifest presence of the Lord was thick, for He was greatly pleased.

As I looked around to embrace this atmosphere of love where the Lord was greatly exalted and welcomed, I had my first vision of Jesus and Abba Father. Jesus looked at me and said, "This is how you treat others better than yourself." As I nodded and smiled, Jesus nudged His Father in the shoulder saying, "Dad, look at what they are doing." Joyous sounds echoed from heaven as Jesus and Abba glowed with affection, happiness, and approval of these women.

Tears flooded my eyes as I joined the others in praising and worshiping our Great God. This miraculous display of Christ's love changed me to the very depths of my being. For the first time in my life I worshipped the Lord unhindered and received the full functioning power of His Spirit. Spiritual gifts that had lain dormant for years were awakened. My family had quite a surprise awaiting them upon my return.

The Lord's Heart

Beloved child, come and drink from the well of My love. You will receive a fresh revelation of who you are, and who I am, for I long to reveal the length, height, and depth of My love for you. As you are filled with an extra measure of love to pour into others, watch how their lives will change as they receive that much needed love from Me, through you.

Loving others will fill your heart with abundant joy and true lasting happiness. I love it when you demonstrate unconditional love and accept others who are different from you. My glory and presence will linger longer in atmospheres of agape love. Where My Spirit resides, there is freedom. Because of that freedom, your heart will overflow with hope and joy. My love covers all of your sins. A cleansed heart allows you to love yourself and others like I love you.

Society overlooks and discards those who don't measure up to their standards. Many who are disabled feel rejected by society and unloved by Me because of their unhealed disabilities. Many become angry with Me, and assume I don't love them. That's not true. I don't show favoritism. My love is abundantly showered over all My children without exception.

As you worshipped Me, I opened your eyes to see past earth's limitations and you saw this precious child of Mine dancing on her feet in complete freedom without her earthly limitations, because there are no wheelchairs in heaven.

Beloved, love never fails! Love bears all things, believes all things, hopes all things, and endures all things. Remember to visit with Me often at My well of love, so you don't run dry. I love you, Abba.

Do nothing from selfishness or empty conceit, but with humility of mind regard one another as more important than yourselves; do not merely look out for your own personal interests, but also for the interests of others.
Philippians 2:3-4

Declaration

I will choose to view others better than myself.

Prayer

Abba Father, help me to view others better than myself. Help me to honor our differences that make us unique. May I extend understanding and patience to others who are slower or different than me. Holy Spirit, cause me to slow down and take notice of those who seem to be discarded by society and make conversation with them. Keep me from thinking I am better than anyone else for You show no partiality and neither will I. Keep me humble. In Christ our Lord. Amen.

His Heart for Me

Are there others in your life that you think less of because they are disabled or not as gifted as you in some areas? Decide in advance to honor and respect them. Don't be in a hurry to go and do the things you think are more important. Look around and make eye contact with others. Ask the Lord how you can view others better than yourself and record it here.

Day 31

Multiplied Blessings

And I will make you a great nation, And I will bless you,
And make your name great; And so you shall be a blessing;
And I will bless those who bless you, And the one who curses you I will curse.
And in you all the families of the earth will be blessed.
Genesis 12:2-3

Thought for the Day: The Lord has blessed me, and I shall be a blessing to others.

Do you like being a blessing to others? I do. There is so much sadness, depression, and anxiety in our world, but the best remedy is Jesus.

In 2 Corinthians 1:4, Paul reminds us that Christ comforts us in all our afflictions, so we can comfort others in all their afflictions. God pours abundant blessings on us, so we can bless others with our overflow. Whatever that overflow might be for you, put it to good use. In Paul's letter to the Galatian Christians, he exhorts them to carry the burdens of their brothers and sisters in Christ for they will be fulfilling the law of Christ. We definitely need others to come alongside us in the midst of our trials and pains. Others can help shoulder some of the weight by lifting us up in prayer, offering a listening ear and sound biblical advice, when appropriate.

When I go through a drive-through, I like to buy the food or drink for the people behind me. Sometimes the Lord will give me a word to share and the person at the drive-through window has the opportunity to pass it along. My obedience not only blesses me, but others as well. It starts a ripple effect where the person behind me buys for the person behind them and so on.

God has blessed us with so much in this nation. Many of us have gifts that could be a blessing to others. Are we using those gifts to their fullest ability? As we are generous with our resources, including our time, it produces the fruit of gratitude and thanksgiving in us for all God has done. As God pours out His grace and mercy upon us, may we be devoted to blessing the world around us as He directs our path.

The Lord's Heart

I will pour out abundant blessings on those who pursue Me with all they have. Those who pursue Me, and not just the gifts or ministries I bestow. Those who hunger and thirst for more of Me will receive the "more" they hunger for. Blessed are those who hunger and thirst for righteousness, for they shall be satisfied. Blessed are the pure in heart, for they shall see Me. Every good and perfect gift is a blessing from above coming down from Me, your Father of the heavenly lights. My blessings to you are strength and help in your time of need. My righteous right hand holds you up and saves you.

The fruit of the Spirit are gifts from Me, blessings you need to walk in the fullness of Christ. You will be blessed when you pray, fast, and give for you have searched My heart, says the Lord, and you have found Me. When My children search for Me and My ways, it is pleasing to Me. When they search for My answer concerning a matter instead of going their own way, this I delight in! This is the kind of heart connection, respect, and love I long for.

Many are stumbling around in busyness forgetting to look to Me. Slow down, My child, and take time to sit at My feet. My blessings shall be like heaven's dew in abundance upon you, bringing you much happiness, spiritual wealth, and protection from all your enemies.

Let us not lose heart in doing good,
for in due time we will reap if we do not grow weary.
Galatians 6:9

Declaration

I will bless Him today with all that I have.

Prayer

Abba Father, empower me to brighten the day of others with a smile or conversation. Thank you for all the abundant blessings You have bestowed upon me. I will not keep these blessings to myself but use them to bless others, which blesses You, Father. Holy Spirit, open my eyes to see those hurting folks around me. Activate Your heart of compassion and love within me, moving me to take action and express love. Help me to realize all that I am and all I have can be a blessing to others, if I am willing.

In Christ our Lord. Amen.

His Heart for Me

Do you have a habit of pursuing gifts and ministries or Jesus? Does your time with the Lord get squeezed out by work, family, or chores? Don't feel bad! Just carve out a few minutes a day to sit with Jesus. He doesn't have rules about how much time we spend with Him, we do. Ask Jesus how you can be a blessing to others and wait for His reply. Record His reply here and take action.

Day 32

Priorities – Who Comes First?

Cease striving and know that I am God.
Psalm 46:10

Thought for the Day: Let go and stop striving.

A couple of years ago my husband and I knew that we had been called to start our own ministry—to help others grow in their relationship with Jesus. In the churches we have attended, we have served in various capacities including children's church, prayer groups, even cleaning. You name it, we've done it. Serving your pastor and the church body is a wonderful blessing to you and others. However, after serving in our church for about a year, we started to resent it. It became a chore and our own duties at home were being neglected like collecting firewood to keep our family warm. Then we started doing street ministry, as well as serving in the church. We were exhausted and annoyed with any additional request for serving. At times both of us felt we needed to perform and serve others to make God happy, but really, we were just making people happy while God was saying, "Rest, My child. You don't have to do all of that."

We had to learn to say, no. Learning to value our time with God and family over serving others is an important lesson. I discovered that many things on my to do list needed to be erased and handed over to others. Because I love being busy about His Kingdom work, it took time to let go of the good things I was doing for Him. My quality time with God was getting pushed out by ministry and life. As a result, my relationship with Jesus was suffering. We desperately need quality time with Jesus to thrive in this life on earth.

From the moment your feet touch the floor, He wants to help prioritize your responsibilities for the day. Surrender your day to His leading and seek to put Him first. Then continue to have an awareness of His presence throughout your day. Jesus is standing by with outstretched hands offering His discernment and boundary-setting tools to bring order to your time. Reach out and accept these precious gifts cloaked in His grace as you learn to put Him first.

The Lord's Heart

Be a good steward of your time. Who will teach your kids about My Kingdom if you are too busy building up others? Don't forget the beloved children I put in your care. By teaching them My ways you will reach more than you know. When you serve, remember to serve with a happy heart as if you are serving Me. Be wise and take care of your own family's needs and take good care of yourself. Don't neglect your time with Me. I would rather you spend time with Me than rushing all around doing ministry stressed out. Many people called to the ministry burn out quickly because they forget to schedule time to be with Me. Your soul and spirit will need refreshing after doing ministry. Spend time with Me in the quiet like Jesus did and I will sustain you and keep you from burnout. You only have so many hours in the day. There are some things that you are doing that are good, but they need to go. Time to hand it off.

Therefore be careful how you walk, not as unwise men but as wise, making the most of your time, because the days are evil.
Ephesians 5:15-16

Declaration

I will set my priorities in order according to God's order of importance.

Prayer

Abba Father, before I place my feet on the ground each morning I will submit my life to Your leading for the day. Assist me in knowing the order of importance for all my responsibilities. May I keep to Your perfect order. Guilt and condemnation from not fulfilling people's expectations be removed from me, in Jesus' name. Holy Spirit, speak words of rest to my soul. Create times of resting and make me aware of them so I can soak in the love of my heavenly Father. I adore You! I long to be with You, Jesus.

In Christ our Lord. Amen.

His Heart for Me

Making a list of your responsibilities will help you determine if you really want to mentor one more person or serve any more than you already do. My list helped me to say "no" where I needed to say "no" so my relationship with God and my family didn't suffer. Be easy on yourself as you seek to put Jesus first. Ask Him what can be eliminated from your list and record it here.

Day 33

Unexpected Love

But I say to you, love your enemies and pray for those who persecute you.
Matthew 5:44

Thought for the Day: True and undefiled love moves you to action.

God's love for you will change your life. My favorite chapters about love in the Bible are 1 John 4 and 1 Corinthians 13. These chapters not only tell us how we are to love others but how God loves us. I personally have 27 pink-colored hearts over the words "love" in chapter 4 of 1 John.

The word "love" has four different meanings in the Greek language: eros, (romantic love), phileo, (enjoyment, fondness, friendship) storge, (family loyalty) and agape, (unconditional love). Today we will focus on agape and phileo love.

Agape love is the love of choice, the love of serving with humility. It is unconditional and intentional. Agape is the highest and purest form of love. It is a divine love not motivated by superficial appearance or emotions.

In 1 John 3:16, the word "agape" is used to describe how Jesus laid His life down for us. It is the most radical form of love, the kind of love that moves you to action not because it feels good, but because it is the loving thing to do. This kind of love is not by impulse or feelings, it is an act of our will. Why does the Lord command us to love our enemies? Because it is a deliberate choice regardless of our feelings.

Phileo means brotherly love, the love between friends. In John 11:36, the word "phileo" is used to describe how Jesus loved Lazarus. This love is more of a strong liking or strong friendship. We don't love our enemies with phileo love because we don't "like" them. However, we can love them with agape love, choosing to show them unconditional love.

Driving through a Wal-Mart parking lot, I noticed two homeless men. As I turned the corner, the Lord said, "Go talk to them."

"What?" I replied. "One girl and two guys, that is not safe. No thanks!" With every pass through the parking lot, I heard the Lord tell me to go talk to them. I wasn't sure if it was the Lord, myself, or the enemy. I was new at hearing the voice of the Lord and needed help and wisdom. I felt a real wrestling in my spirit to obey the Lord. I wanted to obey with every fiber in my being, however, fear was really loud that day.

I wasn't afraid of the homeless men. I was afraid of the condemnation and criticizing judgments I would receive when sharing this experience with others. Honestly, I was trying to reason myself out of obeying the Lord so I could obey man and avoid the comments from those who wouldn't understand. On the last drive by the Lord spoke, "Go talk to them, fear not, for I will protect you and work all things for your good."

"Okay, Lord. I will obey regardless of the consequences, knowing I can trust You."

As I approached the two men, I started talking about Jesus and asked them if they knew Him. They did and talked about Christ like He was their best friend. One had preached before and knew the Bible quite well. As we prayed the Lord's Prayer together, I noticed many people walking by the three of us. I sensed the presence of angels all around us. We had open conversations about the need for Christ's forgiveness of our sins. Mentioning the need to repent and having our minds changed to what is pleasing to the Lord, stirred their hearts. Before turning to leave, I asked, "What can I do for you?" They asked for gloves because it was rather cold outside. While doing my regular shopping, I purchased gloves for them.

As I returned to the parking lot, I handed them the gloves. One of the men said, "I phileo love you." I didn't know what that meant. The man explained that it was a friendly brotherly love. Both men then proceeded to take out treasures from their pockets. One handed me a tattered gospel tract that he had carried around for years. It had gotten him through hard times. I did not want to take it, but he insisted. In exchange, I gave him a new tract for his loved one.

The other man had children and was gathering gifts for his children for Christmas. He also wanted to share some of his treasures. They were very valuable to him but probably only worth a few dollars. "Thank you. But I can't take your children's Christmas gifts," I replied. He got upset and said, "I can take your gifts, but you can't take my gifts? Then you aren't my friend."

Immediately this reminded me of when Jesus told Peter, "If I do not wash you, you have no part with Me." It seemed that Jesus was directly speaking to me. How could I refuse this act of love? This homeless man told me I was priceless and valuable. This was the first time I had ever heard these words from another person. It moved me to tears knowing that my heavenly Father was talking to me through these men.

I still have my treasures from this first evangelism experience. The greatest treasure wasn't the trinkets or tract but the love they expressed in giving what little they had. This was a God moment I will never forget.

This one divine encounter pushed my family forward into our destiny. We now live a life of love and action wherever we go. Christianity should be a lifestyle of living like Christ every day of the week, not just on Sundays.

It is wise to follow Jesus' plan when going out to minister. Jesus sent them out in twos, but occasionally He might ask you to speak to someone when you are alone. If this is a direct command from the Lord, like it was for me, you can be sure that He will protect you. When you are out ministering on the streets, it is wise to stay in well-lit areas with other people around you. And make it a habit to pray with your eyes open for your safety.

The Lord's Heart

Love all My children, even those who don't smell good and aren't living a pleasing life to Me. Love them because I love them. Help them because I want to help them. Remember that you are My hands and feet on earth. When you take time to talk to others and shower them with My love, you make their life better for a time. You give them hope for a life of happiness in Me. When you take time to listen to their needs and problems you make them feel important, noticed, and human. You will do well to not give cash to the homeless on the streets. Give them something they need. Do they need a coat? You have more than one coat, don't you? You could give them a coat. Are they hungry? Buy them some food. Feed and clothe those who ask. If they need gas to get to the next town, pay for a tank of gas. You express My love to others by your actions, beloved. From a place of rest, go and express your love for Me as you help others.

Above all, keep fervent in your love for one another,
because love covers a multitude of sins.
1 Peter 4:8

Declaration

Love is our greatest weapon.

Prayer

Abba Father, may the love I currently have for others increase. Help me to love like You do. Encourage me to slow down and really listen to the testimonies and experiences of others seeking to encourage them and bring them comfort, with the comfort with which I have been comforted. Holy Spirit, draw me to those who are contemplating suicide, those who feel unlovable, and fill my mouth with words from heaven to speak to them. Words that touch their hearts because You love them. Words that convey they are valued in heaven and on earth, and how You would miss them if they ended their lives. In Christ our Lord. Amen.

His Heart for Me

Is there anyone in your life that needs to be shown the love of Christ? How about your spouse? Your kids? Do you withhold love from others until they behave in a certain way? How can you demonstrate the love of Christ to those around you? Ask the Holy Spirit for the answers and write down whatever comes up.

Day 34

Your Special Gifts

Pursue love, yet desire earnestly spiritual gifts,
but especially that you may prophesy.
1 Corinthians 14:1

Thought for the Day: My heavenly Father gives good gifts to me.

There seems to be much confusion today concerning spiritual gifts. For a long time, I thought that there were only nine spiritual gifts and the five offices the Lord gave to the church and nothing more, until I searched the scriptures and found many more gifts. With my focus solely on the five offices and trying to understand what I was called to specifically, I missed another part of who God created me to be. It seemed easier to say I was a teacher and operate out of that instead of bouncing from one gifting to another. While trying to literally pick a title that best suited me, I found myself confused and frustrated. When I finally gave up the need to know my gift, He revealed more of my callings. God didn't want me to put myself in a self-labeled box, a box that limited His work in me.

Are you unknowingly doing this to yourself?

Do you function as a teacher or encourager one month and then find yourself in a season of evangelism for another? Maybe you have a pastor's heart and find yourself mentoring. God can give us multiple gifts. Taking a spiritual gifts test is a very helpful tool for uncovering some of your hidden gifts. After taking a spiritual gift test, I discovered another four or five gifts including exhortation, mercy, and giving.

Let's take a look at two men from the Bible and their gifts, and how they used them. Joseph was a Levite from Cyprus, who was called Barnabas, by the apostles. The name Barnabas means Son of Encouragement or

Son of Exhortation. I believe the apostles gave him this name because he encouraged them. In Acts 9, Barnabas is seen encouraging the apostles to not be afraid of Saul as he shared Saul's encounter on the road to Damascus and how after that experience, Saul, now called Paul preached Jesus Christ with boldness. The apostles went from unbelieving, fearful brothers, to Paul's believing, protective brothers by the testimony, truth, boldness, and encouragement Barnabas released in them.

In Acts 11:22-23, Barnabas was sent out to Antioch by the church in Jerusalem, in search of the facts concerning new believers. When he arrives and witnesses the grace of God, Barnabas rejoices and begins to exhort them all to remain true to the Lord. Although Barnabas is known as an apostle and early leader in the Christian church, more focus and attention is given to his other gifts as an encourager, mentor, and missionary.

John Mark helped Paul and Barnabas on their missionary journeys and was a scribe to Peter. Mark had a humble servant's heart and didn't worry about getting the credit. Would we be satisfied with being an assistant or scribe for someone great? Some would not! Are you willing to accept the seemingly smaller assignments from God or are you holding out for the assignments that seem more important to you? What if the gift that seems small to you is the gift by which you bring many into His Kingdom? John Mark's assignment as an assistant, helper, and scribe were very important roles.

Let's not discount any of the gifts God has given us. All gifts are equally important, none better than another. Don't seek the title, pursue opportunities to use the gifts that God has given you. Maybe you are an encourager like Barnabas or a helper like John Mark.

This is a list of all the gifts found in scripture: gifts, spiritual gifts, and gifts to the church. There are many other gifts given by God like craftsmanship and musical talent that are not specifically listed in scripture. However, we do see people operating in these gifts throughout the Bible.

Gifts: (Romans 12:6-8) Prophecy, Serving, Teaching, Exhortation, Giving, Leading, Mercy.
Spiritual Gifts: (1 Corinthians 12:4-11) Word of Wisdom, Word of Knowledge, Faith, Gifts of Healing, Effecting of

Miracles, Prophecy, Distinguishing of spirits, Various kinds of Tongues, Interpretation of Tongues.

Gifts to the church for the building up of the saints: (1 Corinthians 12:28-31, Ephesians 4:8-13) Apostles, Prophets, Teachers, Miracles, Evangelists, Pastors, Gifts of Healing, Helps, Administrations, Various kinds of Tongues.

The Lord's Heart

My Child, why are you spending so much time trying to figure out what you are called to do? I will reveal it in My time. Maybe now is not the right time for you to know, because you are not ready yet. Often, I will conceal your calling until you have matured so you can handle what I have entrusted to you. Other times I will open a door for you to fulfill your calling because your calling will mature you. Focus on loving Me and seeking My face, not an office or title. In My perfect timing, you will succeed and accomplish your destiny for My Kingdom.

You have many great adventures ahead which support the Body of Christ. Be flexible and willing to follow the path I have laid before you. If the church needs an evangelist, you can fulfill that role until others are raised up. If the church needs someone to serve in the children's area, you can fulfill that role. Your willingness to serve My church is a blessing to Me and an asset to them. How I long to hear these words from the lips of My saints, "Here am I, Lord, send me." As you walk the path of obedience, beloved, My presence goes with you.

Get comfortable with the seasons I will bring you through. If I want you to pastor a church for a season, would you be willing? What about cleaning the church and doing nothing else? The church needs more encouragers, those who help others and lift them up. Are you willing to listen to My voice and then speak My message without fear of man? When there is unity in the body, and My people work together, truly the harvest will be great. I hunger to use you, your abundant giftings and talents to reach others. Do not discount the seemingly small things you do. Everything you do is recorded in heaven. Your record of sins has been erased by Christ's sacrifice, but your record of good deeds will be remembered forever.

As each one has received a special gift, employ it in serving one another as good stewards of the manifold grace of God.
1 Peter 4:10

Declaration

I will not keep my gifts to myself but use them to serve others.

Prayer

Abba Father, thank you for giving me such wonderful gifts. I will seek to bless others using my strengths and giftings. Holy Spirit, teach me how to work together in unity and love with others. Keep me from comparing in pride or insecurity. Prepare my heart and mind to receive more gifts from You. I will be flexible and willing to do even the seemingly smaller things You call me to do. Remove the need to have a title from Your children. We give You permission to do what You need to do in our lives to bring us to maturity, for we want to be meat eaters and not milk drinkers only.

In Christ our Lord. Amen.

His Heart for Me

What brings you joy? Write down what you are good at, your giftings and talents, your blessings from God. God also anoints us in areas that don't necessarily bring us joy, in areas we don't feel gifted. If that is true, He is calling you to trust in Him and what He can do through you. Your faith and love for Him will increase during these times. Record His creative ideas about how to use your gifts to serve others.

Day 35

Jesus: Our Perfect Example

Truly, truly, I say to you, he who believes in Me, the works that I do, he will do also; and greater works than these he will do; because I go to the Father.
John 14:12

Thought for the Day: Christ has no body now but yours. No hands, no feet on earth but yours. Yours are the eyes through which He looks compassion on this world. Yours are the feet with which He walks to do good. Yours are the hands through which He blesses all the world.
—Saint Teresa of Avila

Have you ever asked or begged God to heal a person? God has equipped you as a believer to lay hands on the sick and command healing, in Jesus' name. Have you ever asked God to bring salvation to a person in front of you without sharing the gospel because you were too afraid? I have done both of these things. God was patient with me and He will be patient with you. One day He interrupted my begging prayers and said, "Why are you asking Me to do what I have commanded you to do? I have given you the power to heal and the ability to share Christ." My prayers drastically changed after this interaction.

We are to command healing to manifest, open our mouths and communicate salvation, and forgiveness for sins. Who do you think wants to stop you from doing these things? Your enemy, of course. The devil will throw whatever he can at you to get you to back down from speaking and praying for others. God calls us to be bold and walk in the power and authority that He has given us as believers. The enemy whispers that we are powerless. We must choose to stand with God to see the manifestation of His miracles rather than believe the lies of the enemy.

What do you do when you see a homeless person begging for food? Do you buy them something to eat and talk about Jesus with them or do you turn away and ignore them because of your fear? Jesus says in Luke 3 that if we have two coats, (tunics) we are to share with the one that has none and whoever has food is to do the same. The amount of rotten food we throw away every month could feed several hungry people. Jesus was the ultimate servant. He loved everyone and helped them. We are to get involved in people's lives, too. Ask God to show you how to give of your resources and come alongside others to show them the way of Christ.

Time is God's most precious gift to us but we must be wise in how we spend it. Jesus started His day with God, we should do the same before our schedule gets too overloaded. Time spent in God's presence will reap great rewards for the remainder of the day.

What does it mean to "Be like Jesus?" Jesus said that all men would know that we are His disciples by the love we show others. Since we have the mind of Christ, as believers, our "new normal" means we can think like Him and act like Him. Reach out in love today.

The Lord's Heart

You are My hands and feet to the world. My hands that heal. My hands that lift up another and feed the poor. My hands that offer a stranger water or clothing. You are My feet that bring the good news of Jesus Christ. What you have, which is everything that I have, you bring to those around you. You bring your life experiences and victories as well as your hurts and pains. All that you have gone through can help another. Do you know that My Spirit within you shines out peace, joy, and light to everyone you walk by? Because My will is that none shall perish, I always give more than one opportunity to accept Me. I pursue My children in hopes that they will pursue Me. Beloved, you are My mouth to those around you. Use your words to bless, dear child. Let your light be known throughout the earth. You are My loving arms that embrace My children who are in pain and in need of love.

For you have been called for this purpose, since Christ also suffered for you, leaving you an example for you to follow in His steps.
1 Peter 2:21

Declaration

I will purposely be like Jesus to others in His strength, not through my own striving.

Prayer

Abba Father, it is a privilege to be able to continue the work of Christ on earth. What a honor it is to fulfill the Great Commission and live my life pleasing to You, Father. It brings me so much joy to do Your will. Make me effective in being like Jesus to others. Holy Spirit, I ask for a continual filling all the days of my life. I declare that fear shall not hinder me from sharing the gospel. Judgment shall not keep me from feeding the poor. Greediness shall not hinder me from sharing what I have in excess to those in need. Make me an effectual doer of Your written word.

In Christ our Lord. Amen.

His Heart for Me

Where in your life can you be the hands and feet of Jesus? How about with your family, or at your job, or shopping at the grocery store? Do you pray for the sick or injured ones around you? We have the medicine they need. Do you have people in your life who don't know about Jesus? Are you loving them like Jesus would love them and have you shared your testimony? Grab your pen and get with Jesus.

LIVE BY THE
Spirit
If we live by the Spirit, let us also walk by the Spirit.
Galatians 5:25

His Glorious Glory

Then Moses said, "I pray You, show me Your glory!"
Exodus 33:18

Thought for the Day: Pray for God's glory to be manifested in you and in the earth; then watch for the signs and wonders to occur.

God likes to reveal His glory through the work of His hands. When I think of God's glory, I am reminded of how God went before the Israelites in a visible cloud during the day and a noticeable pillar of fire at night. What glory, what love! Can you imagine the confidence and assurance this gave the people in knowing that their great God was with them every step of the way?

God's glory is often manifested in His creation, we just need to be aware and look for it. A few years ago, my daughter was taking ballet lessons three times a week. While she practiced, I would sit in my car reading scripture, singing, praying, and just enjoying the Lord's presence. My van was commonly called the "prayer mobile." One night as I was parked in an abandoned parking lot, I was meditating on a scripture about seeing the Lord's glory. I prayed out loud, "Lord, show me Your glory, show me Your face. Oh, right, no one can see Your face and live, alright, just show me Your glory." Before I even finished saying the word "glory" a very large deer leaped across the road. Actually, it soared through the air. There had been no deer there before, and none after, I saw just that one. This simple act of showing me His glory moved me to tears.

Another time my son and I went out to our forest to spend some time with the Lord together. We laid out blankets and listened to beautiful music and asked God to be with us. As we rested, my son was having his own wonderful experience with the Lord. I enjoyed watching the Lord speak to him so clearly through His creation. I kept waiting and looking for the Lord to speak to me specifically but was content with watching my son's experience.

Then suddenly God opened the heavens over me and crystal-clear glitter sparkles rained down. I got up and moved around a bit and could still see the glitter-like dust falling on the place I had been. I went back, laid down, and for fifteen minutes the Lord's glory rained down on me. It was absolutely beautiful. He spoke volumes to my heart that day as well as my son's heart through the constant soaring birds over him. You, too, can experience the glory of the Lord. Open your heart and ask God to show you His glory.

The Lord's Heart

All My children shall experience and see My glory. It won't be a one-time experience years ago at a revival meeting or conference or once a week at church during worship. No, My children can live in My glory in the privacy of their homes when they take time out of their busy schedules to sit with Me and pray. When My children take time to walk with Me, I will manifest myself to them. My presence will empower you to live for Me and not for yourself. Moses wouldn't go forward without My presence. Will you go about your day without acknowledging Me? My glory is all around you, dear one. Share My presence with the world. There are many who are depressed and lonely needing a touch of My glory. You carry Me with you. Reach out to that one who looks sad and depressed. It could not only change their life but save their life.

My glory is heavy and powerful. My glory resurrects, delivers, and transforms. My glory is in you twenty-four hours a day. Take time to ponder on that truth. Gaze into the heavens for you shall see My glory if you will but look with eyes of faith. Moses asked to see My glory, you can ask, too, My child. I will reveal My glory to you in a way that will make sense to you. I long to manifest My glory through you and to you, beloved.

But we all, with unveiled face, beholding as in a mirror the glory of the Lord, are being transformed into the same image from glory to glory, just as from the Lord, the Spirit.
2 Corinthians 3:18

Declaration

I will glorify Jesus with my words and actions.

Prayer

Abba Father, thank you for being willing to show me Your glory. I feel honored and loved that You would even consider doing this for me. You hold the universe in Your hands. You want to communicate with me. Help me to grasp that privilege. May I seek to exalt Jesus and bring Him glory in all that I do and say. May Your glory continually fall upon me and may I reflect You everywhere I go. Fill my tabernacle with Your glory for Your glory is as radiant as the most precious jewel, as clear and pure as a heavenly crystal. Holy Spirit, remove the scales from my eyes so I can see God's glory all around me. In Christ our Lord. Amen.

His Heart for Me

Have you ever asked God to reveal His glory to you? Not so you can have a cool story but just to meet with Him and feel close? I encourage you to ask God to reveal His glory to you and watch and see what He will do. Don't feel He doesn't love you if He doesn't reveal His glory right away, be patient in the waiting and rest in His love. Ask in faith, no doubting allowed!

____

____

____

My Beloved

Day 37

Discernment not Judgment

You know of Jesus of Nazareth, how God anointed Him with the Holy Spirit and with power, and how He went about doing good and healing all who were oppressed by the devil, for God was with Him.
Acts 10:38

Thought for the Day: We too have been anointed by the Holy Spirit and have the power to heal and set the captives free.

Spiritual discernment is not a gift for the purpose of judging others. It is a gift that perceives the spiritual realm around us and in us. Every born again believer has a certain level of spiritual discernment. As the believer matures, their discernment will grow. While we are growing in holy discernment, we will need to be careful to not let the log in our own eyes distort our heavenly vision.

Discerning spirits is a great threat to your enemy, the devil. It is the second greatest tool in your toolbox, with love being the greatest gift of all. You can perceive what is from God, the world, the flesh, and the devil. Many of God's children don't know how to use this gift effectively. This gift from the Holy Spirit lets us know when demon spirits or angelic beings are present. We have the ability to know what kind of spirit is operating in us, in others, in meetings, and in words spoken. God will use all of our senses to help us perceive Him and His heavenly realm as well as the demonic realm around us.

To discern correctly, we must use the mind of Christ that God has given us. The fear of being deceived will not be an issue when we abound in love for others. When we discern out of suspicion and fear, our discernment is not clear. Too often God's children get stuck seeing only what the enemy is doing. We are fixated on the negative and bad circumstances around us.

Our enemy can get a hold of this gift and use it against us resulting in us being unbalanced in our discernment. But we must persevere and press in to see what the Lord is doing and hear what the Holy Spirit is saying. Don't give up until you see the good.

Here are some signs you might have the gift of discerning of spirits.

Do you have a longing to see people free from demonic bondage?
Do you want to be more effective in prayer?
Are you sensitive to the spiritual atmosphere? (The glory of God and the yuck of demons?)
Do you have unusual events or manifestations in dreams, visions, or sensations that alert you to the spiritual realm?
Have you seen demons?
Have you seen angels?
Can you sense when something is off?
Can you spot deceptive doctrines?
Do you have a heightened awareness of God's presence and His anointing?

If you find yourself saying yes to these statements, it is very likely that you have the distinguishing of spirits gift, beloved. It is a wonderfully effective gift. The ability to distinguish between spirits is not a curse from God, as some believe, but it is a curse to the devil and he knows it.

The Lord's Heart

When you perceive a demonic spirit, My Holy Spirit will enable you to pray effectively and cause the unholy spirit to leave. Remember to not linger on what the enemy is doing. I allow you to feel oppression in an atmosphere, so you can break its influence by your light and prayer. This gift is very effective when you're engaged in spiritual warfare. My heart aches because My children keep looking at what the devil is doing and come into agreement with him instead of standing against the enemy through prayer by My authority.

My children misuse this gift by criticizing and tearing people down in the name of "discernment." I want to give My children more understanding concerning this great gift. I intended the gift of discernment to be used to set people free from the devil. This gift is not given so you can see the sins of your siblings and point your finger. Pray unceasingly for your brothers and sisters in Christ. When I give the gift of discernment, I give it fully perfected and balanced.

Take notice of the demonic things that are revealed to you and pray by the leading of My Spirit, keeping your focus on what I am doing. Look more intently for My angels working around you and partner with the great I AM. Call My will into existence. Keep your focus on Me and the heavenly realm above. That which you look for, you find, My child. Look for Me.

For to one is given the word of wisdom through the Spirit, and to another the word of knowledge according to the same Spirit; to another faith by the same Spirit, and to another gifts of healing by the one Spirit, and to another the effecting of miracles, and to another prophecy, and to another the distinguishing of spirits, to another various kinds of tongues, and to another the interpretation of tongues.

1 Corinthians 12:8-10

Declaration

I can discern the difference between good and evil.

Prayer

Abba Father, thank you for the power gift of discerning of spirits. Holy Spirit, teach me to keep this great gift balanced and know the power it holds in demolishing our enemy. If I am or become unbalanced and have only the discernment of demons, open my eyes and bring an awareness to the angels at work around me. I ask for great protection over this gift in my life. I declare my vision shall be pure and holy. Grant me wisdom and understanding in knowing the right course of action when I discern angels and demons. In Christ our Lord. Amen.

His Heart for Me

What are your eyes focused on? What is your first response when you walk into a room, do you look to see what the enemy is doing so you can take authority? This is not necessarily bad. However, if you do this every time out of habit, you might become an unbalanced discerner. I encourage you to ask God about His agenda for the day and jump on board with what He shows you and declare it into the atmosphere.

Day 38

Affecting Your Atmosphere

Behold, I have given you authority to tread on serpents and scorpions, and over all the power of the enemy, and nothing will injure you.
Luke 10:19

Thought for the Day: When God's people are standing in their authority, atmospheres will shift and darkness will flee.

Are you sensitive to what's happening when you enter a room? When I walk into a room, I can feel God's presence if godly prayers have been released, or sadness, tension, and despair if negativity is present. The atmosphere's temperature let's me know what kind of words have been spoken. If the words were uplifting and full of life, it feels light and comfortable. If the words spoken were negative and critical, it feels heavy and icky. This is discernment in action.

Many times I thought it was just me being strange. I didn't understand why I immediately felt sick or got a headache when walking into a room. The Lord was trying to show me what was going on in the atmosphere I occupied, so I could pray. He was giving me clues in my body to alert me to the spiritual forces around me.

Do you know that there are principalities and spiritual forces at work everywhere? We don't need to worry or fear these evil forces because our God is greater and He has given us power over the enemy.

Remember your position, child of God. You are seated in the heavenly places with Christ and rule from above, not below. (Ephesians 2:6) Ask the Lord what to do about what you are discerning in the atmosphere. He has a plan. Pay attention to what you sense and feel, so you can pray effectively for your own protection, and for the people you encounter. Our greatest weapons in changing the atmosphere around us are forgiveness and love.

The Lord's Heart

When you walk into a room, dear child, My presence within you makes the darkness flee. Do you realize the power you have within you? You are a carrier of My presence. You can shift atmospheres where darkness resides, places where evil spirits have taken up residence. It is I who lives in you that accomplishes this change around you. Welcome My Spirit in every place you go. Wherever you place your feet, ask Me to send My Spirit and deliver people from bondage. You will see change, dear child, if you pray. Your prayers need not be long. "Come Holy Spirit and deliver" will be enough. You don't have to do battle, just come in authority knowing who is boss in every environment.

Many think they must battle evil spirits. If you know your authority and stand firm in My strength and power, they shall flee from you. Many pray long and loud threatening prayers, but this isn't needed and sometimes the devil is laughing. The devil knows you are trying to convince yourself and not really standing in your God-given power and authority. I have given you the same power and authority over sickness, disease, and evil spirits that I gave My Son. The same power that raised Christ is within you. Now, go and pray. Be attentive and surrendered to Me. I will do amazing things through you.

The Spirit of the Lord God is upon me, Because the Lord has anointed me To bring good news to the afflicted; He has sent me to bind up the brokenhearted, To proclaim liberty to captives And freedom to prisoners.
Isaiah 61:1

Declaration

Everywhere I step, the presence of Christ that dwells within me changes every negative or dark atmosphere.

Prayer

Abba Father, thank you for rescuing me from darkness. Thank you for pulling me out of the pit I was in. You are my everything. You are the breath and substance I need every day. I can't live without You, Lord. Thank you for making me sensitive to Your Spirit and the spirits operating around me. Help me to know the feelings and thoughts that are mine and those that are not, so that I may have wisdom to pray effectively. I declare that I will seek Your counsel and instruction concerning the heaviness I might be feeling. Holy Spirit, empower me to stand and enforce the victory of the cross far and wide! In Christ our Lord. Amen.

His Heart for Me

Are you sensitive to the environment when you walk into a place? Do you sometimes get unexplained headaches or confusion? This can be a sign of witchcraft. Take note of the things you feel and sense that aren't part of your normal life and ask the Lord what to do. He may want you to pray something through or bring deliverance to that environment. Let Him choose the way He wants to do it. Record what He reveals here.

Day 39

Seeing in the Spirit

But blessed are your eyes, because they see; and your ears, because they hear.
Matthew 13:16

Thought for the Day: The man who has been taught by the Holy Spirit will be a seer rather than a scholar. —A. W. Tozer

---

God has given His children the ability to see both with our physical eyes and our spiritual eyes. This gift is given to both adults and children. Our responsibility is to nurture and develop this gift. Many people can see well with their physical eyes, but their spiritual sight is dim.

One of Paul's prayers for the Philippian believers was that their love, knowledge, and depth of insight would abound still more. (Philippians 1:9) This is my prayer too. Some people are born with the ability to see fully in the spirit, meaning they can easily see angels, demons, and other spiritual beings, while others must develop their seeing abilities with the Lord's help. Paul knew the importance of spiritual sight. He not only prayed for the believers in Philippi but for the believers in Ephesus. (Ephesians 1:17-18) Paul wanted all of God's children to have the eyes of their hearts (our inner person) enlightened so we can "see" without using our physical eyes. Spiritual insight deepens our relationship with the Triune God and all His heavenly hosts.

To see into the spirit realm means to simply see things as if they were there when they are not in the physical world where they can be touched. In 2 Corinthians 4:18, we are told to fix our eyes on what is unseen (eternal), instead of what is seen (temporary). What is eternal? God, Christ, Holy Spirit, heaven, angels, everlasting life, joy, and peace. How can we fix our eyes on what is unseen? When we read the scriptures and spend time with God, our vision improves so we can set our eyes on what is unseen.

Parents and grandparents of young children, teach your little ones to pray. If they are sensing or seeing something scary in their room, teach them to tell the scary things to leave in the name of Jesus. Teach them that Jesus is the light and that all darkness must flee when they call out Jesus' name. Cultivate that kind of faith in those God has entrusted in your care.

If children are told that what they are sensing, seeing, and feeling is made up and not real, they may be shut off from their gift because they believe their minds are lying to them. When I was a child, this happened to me. This caused me to lose the ability to see the dark evil things in my room, which was a huge blessing, but also shut me off from seeing the lovely angels of God for over 30 years. God restored my spiritual sight a few years ago. The lies I once believed were replaced with His truth and my ability to see in the spirit increased.

A practical way to increase your spiritual sight and fix your eyes on what is unseen is to open up your bible and start picturing what you read. Picture yourself with Jesus, walking along the sea of Galilee. Imagine yourself in the boat with the rest of the disciples as Jesus calmed the storm. God will increase and develop your seeing abilities as you follow this practice. Remember, His Word is alive, active, and full of power.

The Lord's Heart

Those of you who are My children and believe in Me can see in the spirit, hear in the spirit, and walk by the spirit. My Spirit enables you to live this way. I want to have conversations with you like I did with Adam and Eve. We spoke spirit to spirit, face to face. This is My desire for you. Don't run from prophetic person to prophetic person wanting to hear a word or vision from Me, seek Me for the vision and revelation you desire. You, too, can see and hear. This will take effort and practice on your part, but it is worth it. On the day of Pentecost, I poured out My Spirit on all flesh. I will give you visions and dreams. You will hear My voice and prophesy.

Ask Me for wisdom concerning the things I am showing you and write down what you see. I will give you revelation about My Kingdom, about who I am and who you are, not only through My Word but through your own experiences. If you want to have pure eye gates, when seeing in the spirit, you will need to allow the Holy Spirit to be your filter. I will inform you when I am grieved concerning the things you watch and read, says the Spirit of the Lord. Be sensitive to My nudge and trust Me in My request. I want you to see and hear in the spirit, so you can pray and intercede for what I am revealing to you. Every child of Mine has spiritual sight that can be activated and matured. Be bold and call it forth! Together we will accomplish My purposes on earth.

By faith he left Egypt, not fearing the wrath of the king;
for he endured, as seeing Him who is unseen.
Hebrews 11:27

Declaration

I will use my spiritual eyes to look for what He will uncover to me.

Prayer

Abba Father, thank you for giving Your children the ability to see, hear, and walk in Your Spirit. I ask for an increased awareness to the ways of Your Spirit. Give me wisdom and understanding about the things I am seeing. I declare I will not be afraid of my ability to see but learn and grow in it. Holy Spirit, enlighten the eyes of my heart and increase all my spiritual senses. Assist me in protecting my eye gates from unholy things for I want my vision to be pure, undefiled, and full of light.

In Christ our Lord. Amen.

His Heart for Me

Do you take time to see in the spirit? Can you sense when angels are around or can you actually see them? Do you know when there is an evil presence in the room because you feel, smell, or see it? Ask the Lord specific questions about the things you see and wait for His answers. Ask Him what it means and what your responsibility is in being allowed to see it.

Day 40

Our Divine Prayer Partner

In the same way the Spirit also helps our weakness; for we do not know how to pray as we should, but the Spirit Himself intercedes for us with groanings too deep for words.
Romans 8:26

Thought for the Day: Praying in tongues will enlighten and strengthen you.

Praying is an honor and a privilege, but it is also hard work. Do you ever wonder how to pray? Do you ever run out of things to pray about? We have an amazing helper. The Holy Spirit helps us pray when we don't know what to pray. (Romans 8:26) Sometimes it's challenging to pray the Father's will correctly over friends and family because we usually have an idea of what they need or want. Frequently what they want is not the Father's will.

One day the Lord radically changed my prayer time when I sat down to pray for an hour. "Lord, there are too many needs. I just don't know where to start." My heart's desire was for my prayers to be effective and to pray what He wanted me to pray. Going down a list of names, doesn't feel honoring to me or very productive. I long to connect to the Father's heart and pray from that place of intimacy.

The Lord told me to pray in the spirit, so I did. What happened next surprised me. I didn't pray from my prayer list, God said He had others taking care of those prayers. He needed me to pray in the spirit for a girl in another country who was in danger. After about 15 minutes of praying in tongues, the Lord showed me I was praying for a young Asian woman who was being followed by two men who had evil intentions in their hearts. It was an intense time of intercession.

In the natural, I told her to run, and she ran. Then to turn left, and she turned. After 30 minutes of prayer, she finally made it to safety. I flowed from tongues to English through a very real vision that played like a movie before me. This happened three years ago but I still remember all the details.

There are many benefits to praying in tongues. Here are a few of them. When you pray in tongues you are addressing the Father in a language no one can understand but Him unless He gives you or someone else the interpretation. (1 Corinthians 14:2) Speaking in tongues is also used as a means of spiritual edification. The word edify means "to build up." (1 Corinthians 14:4) For me, it's like a secret prayer between me and Abba. If this gift has lain dormant in you for a few years, ask the Lord to revive it for His Kingdom purposes. If you want to receive the gift of speaking in tongues in order to strengthen and edify yourself, ask Jesus to baptize you in the Holy Spirit. He loves to see you empowered.

Connect to Abba Father's heart and pray accordingly. He might just surprise you with His own prayer burdens. Make yourself available today and see what He will do. Your prayers may save a life.

The Lord's Heart

Do you know the prayer partner you have within you? The Holy Spirit knows everything about Me and everything about you. When you ask the Holy Spirit to join you in prayer, do you know the wisdom and power that is released in that prayer time? He knows exactly what to pray. He knows exactly what time to pray. Holy Spirit will wake up those who are willing to pray with Him at any hour. Are you waking up at 2 a.m. and having a hard time falling back to sleep? Have you considered that I might want to talk to you? There might just be someone who needs your prayers. If I want to wake you up, are you willing? Be willing! "The Spirit Himself intercedes for you with groanings too deep for words." Holy Spirit is always two steps ahead of the devil and knows the outcome of everything before you do. He has great wisdom therefore you have great wisdom! Get in line and keep in step with Him, praying all He tells you to pray.

For if I pray in a tongue, my spirit prays, but my mind is unfruitful.
What is the outcome then?
I will pray with the spirit and I will pray with the mind also;
I will sing with the spirit and I will sing with the mind also.
1 Corinthians 14:14-15

Declaration

I can pray the Father's will for I have His Spirit within.

Prayer

Abba Father, I am eternally grateful for Your Spirit. Thank you for the help that He is to me. Bring an awareness to all your children of just how precious the Holy Spirit is. He is not the weird uncle to be avoided but the very heart of who You are. Holy Spirit, blow and uncover all the lies that have been spoken about You. Flush out the counterfeit spirits masquerading around confusing Your children and bringing fear. Bring healing truth to those who have seen this unholy spirit at work and heard it being called, the Holy Spirit. In Christ our Lord. Amen.

His Heart for Me

Do you have the gift of tongues? If so, pray in the spirit daily. Don't put demands on how long, etc. Just enjoy connecting to the Father's heart through His Spirit. Have you ever tried singing in the spirit? Give it a try. When praying in tongues, ask the Lord for the interpretation. Many times He is just waiting for you to ask. Record what the Spirit of the Lord reveals. Make memories with the Spirit today.

Day 41

Ministering Angels

But when we cried out to the Lord, He heard our voice and sent an angel.
Numbers 20:16

Thought for the Day: The Lord commands His angels concerning you.

Angels are worshippers - they worship God and His Son, Jesus, every day for all of eternity! Thousands upon thousands of angels surround His throne saying in a loud voice, "Worthy is the Lamb that was slain to receive power and riches and wisdom and might and honor and glory and blessing." The angels rejoice when one sinner repents and accepts Jesus, there is a great celebration in heaven. God's angels are always near us and they join us as we worship God on earth.

For many years I ignored angels, fearing that I would unknowingly worship them or elevate them above Jesus. During this time, I started having numerous visions of angels especially when I was worshipping the Lord. I couldn't avoid them any longer. God began to speak to me through the angels. I was to partner with them to bring God's will to the earth.

In a vision God said to me, *It is okay to study My angels and their ministry to you. I like it when you study My Word to learn about My Kingdom and what is available to you. Study how My people interacted with them. I will give you discernment about what is pleasing to Me. Just be willing and open to learning about all of My Kingdom. Allow Me to stretch your understanding.*

My first question as I dove into scripture was: "How do angels minister to us?"

Angels strengthen us and sometimes feed us. In Matthew 4:11, we see angels ministering to Jesus. They provided Him with food and water like they did for Elijah in 1 Kings 9:5-8. They supernaturally strengthened Jesus for His ministry and Elijah for his journey. In the Garden of Gethsemane, we see an angel comforting and strengthening our agonizing, precious savior.

Angels help us in evangelism. There was an Ethiopian eunuch coming back from worshipping in Jerusalem who didn't know Jesus. An angel of the Lord spoke to Philip telling him to "Go, south" because there was a eunuch that needed understanding of the scriptures. (Acts 8:26-39) Because Philip obeyed the voice of the angel, and the Holy Spirit, another soul entered the kingdom of God.

Angels protect, warn, and deliver us from our enemies. An angel of the Lord appeared to Joseph in a dream and said, "Get up! Take the child and His mother and flee to Egypt and remain there until I tell you; for Herod is going to search for the child to destroy Him." (Matthew 2:13)

The angel of the Lord encamps around those who fear Him, And rescues them. (Psalm 34:7)

My God sent His angel and shut the lions' mouths and they have not harmed me. (Daniel 6:22)

Now I know for sure that the Lord has sent forth His angel and rescued me from the hand of Herod and from all that the Jewish people were expecting. (Acts 12:11)

We must use wisdom and discernment when studying or interacting with angels. Asking angels questions when they appear is not angel worship but it is wise to ask where they are from, knowing that there are fallen angels seeking to lead us astray. Praying to, bowing down before, and elevating angels above Jesus is a form of idolatry and angel worship. This has been an issue since the Apostle Paul's time.

A new issue has arisen within the Body of Christ. It is the thought that our angels are bored because we are not commanding them. When we search the living scriptures, we find no reference to Christians commanding angels. However, if our prayers match the Father's heart and will, God dispatches angels to complete their assignments in answer to our prayers as it says in Hebrews 1:14.

The Lord's Heart

Angels and saints serve Me, says the Lord of Hosts. I have given you the privilege of working with angels. I handcrafted angels to obey and listen to My instructions. I fashioned them to perform that which I want them to perform. They give you instructions to bring about My perfect plan in your life and in the lives of those I send you to help. I send them out to minister in response to your prayers. They fulfill their duties by My word of approval to your prayers and My will concerning matters you are not even aware of. You can ask Me to release angels to help at any given time for My angels are all around you. I have assigned many angels to you, beloved. Their mission is to minister to you through strengthening, warning, protecting, giving insight, and instructions from Me. You are co-laborers with angels bringing My will to the earth. My angels are filled with My plans and will for your life, others, and the earth.

I have powerfully strong angels protecting you from your enemy. Persevere in praying to Me, for I collect every prayer of yours placing them into golden prayer bowls in My throne room. My angels come and mix incense with your prayers laying them on the golden altar before Me. I hear every prayer! Big or small, loud or quiet. It doesn't matter, I hear them all. I command My angels to mix fire with your prayers throwing them to the earth, bringing the answers to your prayers. Pray constantly, beloved. Never let your prayer bowl be empty but keep filling it for I will tip the bowl and pour abundant blessings of health, wealth, and favor upon you. My ways are glorious, says the Lord of Hosts.

Bless the Lord, you His angels, Mighty in strength, who perform His word, Obeying the voice of His word! Bless the Lord, all you His hosts, You who serve Him, doing His will.

Psalm 103:20-21

Declaration

Angels are released when I pray to Abba.

Prayer

Abba Father, thank you for assigning angels to help me. They helped Jesus and they will help me also. Holy Spirit, teach me to cooperate and work with God's angels instead of ignoring them. Increase and mature my spiritual vision so I can see and work with Your heavenly hosts effectively, Lord. Give me confidence in the fact that You release Your angels in response to my prayers. Thank you for the ministry of angels to those who believe. Thank you for their help in evangelism and directing us in the way we should go. Thank you for the protection they give.

In Christ our Lord. Amen.

His Heart for Me

Are you worried that talking to angels will take your focus off Jesus? This is a valid concern, but don't let that stop you from learning all about the kingdom of God. His angels were created to serve Him and part of serving Him is to minister to us. Have you experienced angelic ministry? Tune your ears to the voice of the Holy Spirit and write what He reveals here.

Day 42

Dreaming With God

Jesus answered them, "To you it has been granted to know the mysteries of the kingdom of heaven, but to them it has not been granted."
Matthew 13:11

Thought for the Day: Dreaming is one way the Lord speaks to us.

As a child, I had an active imagination. I daydreamed while I was in school and at home doing my homework. I also dreamed at night. A few negative comments about daydreamers broke my cycle of dreaming. Dreaming was looked upon as a waste of time and foolish by those around me. By the time I was in my late teens, I stopped dreaming all together. I didn't start dreaming again until I turned 40.

Our dreams can come from several different sources: our enemy, our soul, or God. We need discernment to tell the difference between them, and then wisdom from God to decipher the meaning of the dreams He wants us to understand.

God has restored my creative imagination. Had the Lord showed me His plans for my future 10 years ago, I would have laughed. But now, I wait expectantly for the things He has shown me to transpire. Because of my past experience, I don't often share God's big dreams for my future with others. There are many who would laugh, speak negatively over them, and tell me that my dreams will never happen. What many don't understand is that God gives us big dreams for our future because they are part of our future. His plans can make us uncomfortable, because they are bigger than the dreams we have for ourselves.

Don't accept the lies from the enemy that say, dreamers are fools or dreamers waste time. Daniel and Joseph didn't waste time, they saw God's big dreams for them come true. Dream big with God and embrace the future He has for you.

The Lord's Heart

I am raising up My Daniels and Josephs in this hour. Those who dream dreams and can interpret not only their own dreams but the dreams of others. By My Spirit they shall interpret and call people forth into their destinies and give warnings. In My power and wisdom this will be established in the whole earth. Greater discernment will be given to those who have dreams and visions. I will speak a thing and they shall remember. I want to bring revelation to My people. They need to know that I speak to them through their dreams. I am talking to many who don't know Me through their dreams.

Through the night hours, I am drawing them to Me when they are finally at rest. The night hours that have been filled with nightmares, I have taken back as I give My children godly dreams and visions about their futures. Their destiny is planted in the night hours and I conceal the matter until they are hungry and ready to search it out. More of who I am is revealed through dreams and visions just as more of who you are is revealed as you dream with Me. Some revelation will carry responsibility and require action on your part while other revelation will simply deepen our intimacy and friendship. Lean back and dream with Me, says the Lord. Let your imagination flow freely as you rest and dream in My arms.

It is the glory of God to conceal a matter,
But the glory of kings is to search out a matter.
Proverbs 25:2

Declaration

I will record my dreams for God speaks to me through my dreams.

Prayer

Abba Father, thank you for speaking to us through our dreams. Flood my life with godly dreams and visions. Bring to life those big-sized dreams that only You can answer. Holy Spirit, open my eyes and ears to the spiritual realm all around me, even during the day. Reveal prayer strategies in the night. Reveal Your will, Father, for the situations in my life where I need breakthrough. Expose it in the night hours. May I be diligent to keep asking You for understanding while looking at the dream. Dreams that have died due to naysayers and negative people speaking death over them, be restored now! In Christ our Lord. Amen.

His Heart for Me

Before you go to sleep, ask God to give you a dream. Make sure you have a pen and notebook close by to record what He reveals to you. Also, be ready to be woken up at any hour. When you are ready to get up in the morning, ask God for further revelation concerning your dream. Revisit your dreams by looking at them again with God at a later date. For the Lord loves to give us continued revelation about our dreams. Take time to dream with God.

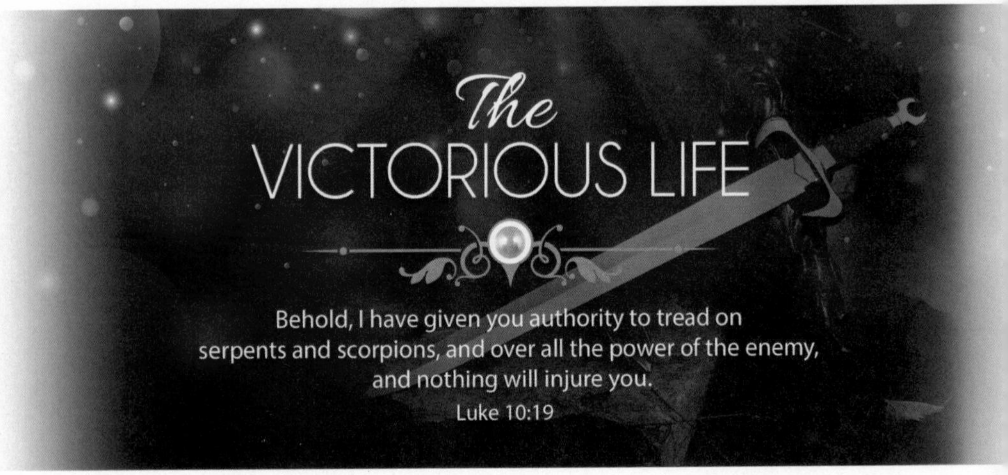
The
VICTORIOUS LIFE
Behold, I have given you authority to tread on serpents and scorpions, and over all the power of the enemy, and nothing will injure you.
Luke 10:19

Day 43

Chin Up

I can do all things through Him who strengthens me.
Philippians 4:13

Thought for the Day: Go, do what God is telling you to do and don't let fear stop you.

As I lay in bed one morning, I felt an overwhelming sense of fear and depression. The Lord was calling me to change—I dreaded the thought. I don't like looking like a fool. The source of my depression and fear was this lie: "I can't do what the Lord is asking me to do."

Comfortable with what I was doing for the Lord, I didn't want to move into the new place He was calling me—"evangelism." Super scary for the shy person who likes to be by herself most days. Being with others has always made me feel uncomfortable. Whenever I went to social gatherings, which I tried to avoid at all costs, I hid in the corner where I felt safe.

Fear was my constant companion. It served me well as a teen when I needed to run to safety. In my twenties, I was determined to put up a wall of protection to avoid being abused or hurt by anyone ever again. Little did I know that as I put up those walls of protection I was building my own prison. It was a prison filled with bitterness, anger, and unforgiveness. I suffered from a "poor me" victim mentality and by choosing to react to people this way, I was miserable. Through the Lord's pruning process, He delivered me from the spirit of fear.

Fear still tries to rear its ugly head, but now I know that the power of Christ in me leaves no room for fear. We can push through fear by doing what makes us afraid.

When we accept thoughts of fear as our own and let them paralyze us, we are in agreement with the devil rather than God's truth. Fear is a spirit of the devil we have to deal with, not live with. 1 John 4:18 says, "Perfect love casts out fear." Be perfected in His love and continually trust in Him. Fear not, beloved.

The Lord's Heart

Step out of the boat where you have put yourself. You think you are safe in the boat, but the boat is holding you back. The boat of protection needs to be abandoned. As you step out of your comfort zone, grab hold of My hand. My hand is stretched towards you, not against you. The great and mighty I AM is waiting for you to grab hold of His hand. Lift your chin, My beloved child, and stare into My eyes, the source of your comfort and joy. I am your protector. You would be astonished to see how I have been protecting you all along the way. I haven't withdrawn My righteous protective hand from you.

Do you remember when Peter took his eyes off Me and looked at the storm? When he allowed the storm to be bigger than Me, Peter started to sink. Peter broke eye contact. As he lost his trust in Me, fear and doubt took over. Trust Me with all that you have and keep your eyes forever on Me and not on the circumstances or people around you. "I have not given you a spirit of fear, but of power and of love and of a sound mind." You will not fear man if you stay focused on Me and My ways. Come walk on water to Me. The storms of life are under your feet. Your ankles might get wet, but you will not be taken down. You will rise above the storm.

Do you feel unworthy of My help? Are you afraid to admit you need help? Trust Me with your life! My plans for your life are better than your own. My love for you is everlasting and not dependent on what you do or don't do. I will keep reaching for you. I will keep guiding you. My right hand will always be under, before, behind, and above you, with the intention of drawing you to Me. Like the mother hen who gathers her chicks and protects her young, I will protect you under My wings.

I call you to things you can't do because you must rely on Me, My strength, and the power of the Holy Spirit to get it done.

I receive great glory from you and others when people see you doing things they never thought you could do. Others will know that all things are possible with Me. I enjoy watching you learn to trust Me more.

And He has said to me, "My grace is sufficient for you, for power is perfected in weakness."
2 Corinthians 12:9

Declaration

I can depend on His strength and power that is within me.

Prayer

Abba Father, thank you that no weapon formed against me will prosper. All chains of fear have been broken through Christ's sacrifice at Golgotha. Hallelujah! I surrender my will to You. Take me outside my comfort zone. I will trust You in the deep and unknown waters of life. Holy Spirit, thank you for empowering me to fully step into my calling, obeying the will of my Father without hindrance. Arise, spirit of life! I am confident Christ can do the impossible in and through me! In Christ our Lord. Amen.

His Heart for Me

Fear is a tool of our enemy to keep us from our destiny. What are you afraid of doing? Are you afraid of looking like a fool? Do you walk in fear of man instead of God? Draw near to the Lord and listen for His instructions on how to remove the fear, push through it, or simply exchange the lie for the truth. Where can you stop agreeing with the devil and start agreeing with what the Lord is saying?

Day 44

Stand in Hopeful Expectancy

But he must ask in faith without any doubting, for the one who doubts is like the surf of the sea, driven and tossed by the wind. For that man ought not to expect that he will receive anything from the Lord.
James 1:6-7

Thought for the Day: Faith is hope in things unseen.

Expectations-we all have them. Unfortunately, what we desire and hope for isn't always what we get in this life.

When our reality, or a person we love, doesn't meet our expectations, our minds can respond in negative ways causing our happiness to decrease and disappointment, anger, complaining, and sadness to rise. This can harm our relationship with God and our relationship with others. Do your friends and family believe they will never measure up to your standards because they overhear you complaining about how they have let you down? Do you unknowingly withhold love thinking that will cause them to change and meet your demands? Oh, how wrong we are. We must choose to love unconditionally because each of us is on our own walk of sanctification.

As a young mother, I had expectations of how my children should behave at home and in public. Now as teenagers, I still have expectations about their decisions and their future career choices. My husband is not exempt. My unrealistic expectations caused me to be frustrated and disappointed in him often. I unknowingly put expectations on God as well. Thinking He should answer my prayers in a certain timeframe and in a certain way. When He didn't answer in the way I hoped, frustration took root. I found myself always looking to see if my expectations were being met, and if they didn't, I became annoyed. Do you ever feel this way?

Having God's standards before our eyes is good but who left us in charge of holding people accountable to God's standards, when we can't even meet His standards ourselves? This is not our job! Our job is to pray that all of God's children, including ourselves, would be pleasing to Him in all things, living up to our full potential in Christ.

Living a life with expectations is simply a belief that someone should achieve something or be a certain way, your way. Expecting others, and even God, to behave in ways that conform to your standards will make you miserable. It is a fruitless, frustrating way to live.

Living a life of expectancy is living a life of hope in what God has promised in scripture. Faith is having a hopeful expectancy that God will answer your prayers. As children of God, we must know what He has promised to us and declare those promises in faith over our lives, and those we love, until they manifest. Learn to live a life of expectancy and see what God will do.

The Lord's Heart

Refrain from weighing My people down with all your expectations. You expect people to come to maturity in the blink of an eye. Sanctification takes time. Have you come to maturity yet? Let Me hold My children to My standards for I am much more patient and enduring than you are. Drop your self-righteous attitude and let Me be the righteous judge of My people. My ways are not your ways, beloved. I have commanded you to love everyone. Start loving those who frustrate you. Pray for those who need to grow in their relationship with Me. I will finish the good work I have started in all My children. Sanctification shall be complete when I return to get you.

It pleases Me when you declare My promises over yourself and others. You can hold Me to them. My promises are part of your inheritance in Christ. They are gifts to you. I shall fulfill My promises to you in My timing so continue to be patient while you wait. Be open to how I want to answer, and when I want to answer, not holding Me to a specific outcome. Will you still love Me when My answer is no? Believe I have something better for you. When My answer is not yet, continue to stand in hope and faith, and remember My faithfulness.

Remain open-minded, dear child. Practice acceptance and grace. Accept yourself and others right where they are in life. My path of sanctification for you and others is overflowing with grace. I'm not bothered by your mistakes. Be willing to change your focus. Look at how far you have come. Look at where you once were and where you are now on the path of sanctification. You have changed and come so far, beloved. So have many others. Perfection is not the key. Transformation over time, one layer at a time is more realistic. Rejoice in your victories. Rejoice in the smallest of changes towards holiness. I love you. Your Beloved King

This is the day which the Lord has made; Let us rejoice and be glad in it.
Psalm 118:24

Declaration

I will continually stand in hopeful expectancy.

Prayer

Abba Father, help me to release all unrealistic expectations I have of myself and others. Help me to extend grace to myself when I make mistakes. Give me Your perspective, Lord. May I have great contentment along my path of sanctification not holding to any mindsets of perfectionism that weigh me down. May I be a person who calls people higher into holiness while embracing the place they currently are. Holy Spirit, empower me to focus on all the good and positive changes that have already occurred in my life and in the lives of those around me. May I speak truth and light into what You have already done, and continue to do in and through us.

In Christ our Lord. Amen.

His Heart for Me

Write down the expectations you place on yourself and others. Are they God's expectations? If they are God's standards, pray and have patience. Remember to extend grace to yourself and others. Make allowances for mistakes. Take all your expectations of what could be, should be, or will be, and talk with Jesus about them all. Grab a cup of coffee or tea and commune with Him. He is waiting to talk with you.

Day 45

Overcoming Your Fears

For God has not given us a spirit of timidity,
but of power and love and discipline.
2 Timothy 1:7

Thought for the Day: Inaction breeds doubt and fear. Action breeds confidence and courage. —Dale Carnegie

What are you afraid of? I have lived with fear for 30 years. It has invaded every area of my life. Fear of the water is something I overcame with God's help. You, too, can overcome your fears!

As a young child, the devil knew my potential and tried to take me out several times by drowning me. At the age of eight, my mom decided to enroll me in swimming lessons after my near-drowning accident in our very deep duck pond. On the last day of lessons, all the kids lined up to jump off the diving board. I wanted to escape but the other kids wouldn't let me. The instructor told me she'd catch me, but I didn't believe her. Due to the fear raging inside of my body, I lost control of my bladder but no one noticed as they pushed me off the diving board.

Sinking to the bottom of the pool, I had an out-of-body experience. Time stood still. I had great peace, no longer fighting to breathe. As I sat on the bottom of the pool, I watched the other kids laughing and pointing their fingers. Where was the instructor? It was like I was watching a movie fully relaxed and not worried. I felt the presence of the Lord while I was down there. The instructor finally came to my rescue, and to everyone's surprise, I wasn't coughing and didn't need any medical attention.

In my later teens I was tormented by the voices of the enemy, but somehow thought they were my own. I unknowingly agreed with the devil that I was worthless and tried to take my own life by water, and other methods. In my twenties, I had a few brave moments trying to swim but they were short lived.

Fear always seemed to keep me out of the water. Our children love to swim and I always felt guilty for not wanting to be in the water with them but I was anxious and fearful. If I couldn't touch the bottom, my body would start reacting in strange ways, ways all born out of fear. I was even afraid to put my face in the shower water.

One day, I had enough! As I begged Christ to help me, I started forcing my face in the water and blowing water out of my nose. I must have looked ridiculous. I coughed and felt like I was choking. I forced myself to go under the water. I thought I was going to go crazy as I pushed through this fear. I thought I'd die, but I didn't want to die anymore.

While doing this at the YMCA, others asked me if I was alright. I explained what I was doing, and they encouraged me to continue. One day a man in a wheelchair showed up who had no legs. He was there to swim. I was so encouraged by this strong man of faith. We talked often and encouraged each other. This was a time of healing and deliverance for me.

I'm still not a strong swimmer, but I gained freedom by pushing through the fear that once held me hostage. If I hadn't faced my fears head on, I would still be in bondage. Whenever fear tries to rise up in our thoughts, we must take that thought captive and make it obedient to Christ. How do we practically do this? We must look at the belief that is causing the fear and replace it with the truth. Ask Christ for a "new" thought to replace the thought that once caused fear. Fear subsides as you speak the truth and then practice the action that once made you afraid. In my case, it was swimming.

Is there some action you need to take to overcome your fear? Jesus will help you discover your plan of action and overcome your fears. I am living proof, His promises are true.

The Lord's Heart

I am your helper, My beloved child. If you will look to Me, I will make you strong. Do not let your heart be troubled or afraid, I am working behind the scenes to help you. Be strong and courageous, do not be afraid. I have commanded you to be courageous and given you My power to face any obstacle and overcome it. Don't accept that fear as your own. Your enemy, the devil, wants to keep you afraid of everything, causing you to be ineffective. You have been redeemed from fear, My peace resides in you. Wear My peace around you like a warm coat insulating you from fear.

You are Mine, I have called you by name. Set your gaze on Me and trust Me, and I will deliver you from fear. The great I AM is always with you. I will never leave you or forsake you, My child, that is the truth. My Spirit gives you power to overcome fear. Call upon the Holy Spirit that resides in you for He is your helper. I AM the Lord your God who takes hold of your right hand and helps you through every fearful circumstance in life. As you hold on tightly, I will lead you out of that fear today.

I sought the Lord, and He answered me,
And delivered me from all my fears.
Psalm 34:4

Declaration

I will not be afraid for I have a mighty
and awesome God fighting for me.

Prayer

Abba Father, bring Your truth upon my head like a helmet of protection from fear. Belt of truth, be tightly fastened around my waist and never loosen! Lies, I rebuke you and cast you into the sea. Be removed from me! I declare that I will purposefully set my mind and heart on the things above. Fear will no longer have a place to operate in my life. Holy Spirit, empower me to stay focused on the things of Christ, not the things of this world. Lasting peace is my forever portion. Saturate me in Your love and peace today, Lord. I want to feel Your overwhelming peace in my life today and forever. I command my nerves and brain to come into alignment with Your will for peace and contentment.

In Christ our Lord. Amen.

His Heart for Me

What are you afraid of? Is your faith in your ability and plans or God's plans? Are you afraid of looking like a fool or being wrong? Are you believing lies that need to be tossed and replaced with the truth? Ask Jesus to reveal the things you are still afraid of and the lies that need to go. Ask Him for help and a plan of action. Speak declarations of truth every day but especially when fear rises up in you.

Day 46

Victorious in Christ

Therefore, take up the full armor of God, so that you will be able to resist in the evil day, and having done everything, to stand firm.
Ephesians 6:13

Thought for the Day: Satan is under my feet.

Anger rose within me, as I stood in his hospital room. My prayers didn't seem to be accomplishing anything. My heart was being torn apart by the current circumstances. I knew prayer to be effective and powerful. We had faith in God to rescue and deliver. We were standing on the promises of God, yet it seemed like the enemy was winning.

One day in total desperation I begged the Lord to give me strategies and wisdom on how to take the devil down in this man's life. I was worn out. What was I doing wrong? Very calmly the Lord said, "Tell the enemy to be silent so I can do what I need to do."

"Is it really that simple?" I asked the Lord.

"Yes, it is really that simple. You've been throwing all kinds of things at the enemy and he has been laughing at you. He has worn you out and caused a lot of pain. You've been running around in circles for quite a while. A few words inspired by Me will take him down."

"Alright, Lord."

I began to pray, "Satan, I command you to be silent in this man's life right now, so God can do what He needs to do. In Jesus' name. Amen."

About ten minutes later, there was major breakthrough! His heart turned towards the Lord again. The man's eyes were opened to the fact that he had been listening to the devil, and obeying him, instead of God. I was completely overjoyed!

Through this experience, I learned that I must not lean on my own understanding, but listen to Jesus and His strategies to defeat the enemy.

In Hebrews 2:14, it is clear that the devil was rendered powerless through Christ's death. However, he will try to gain access to our lives by getting us to agree with him and what he is doing. When we stand in our authority and speak in the power of the Holy Spirit, the devil must flee.

The Lord's Heart

You are victorious! The same power that raised Jesus from the grave is alive in you, He gave it to you. Don't sit back and accept the attacks of the devil but don't fight crazily without understanding. You were made to stand strong and victorious. Being victorious does not mean a life that is always happy for there will be trials and testings bringing pain. The victorious life is one that overcomes every obstacle. You will have scars and stories from the battles you have won.

I am with you even if you have to circle the mountain a couple of times to learn your lesson. If you aren't advancing, at least hold your ground by trusting and declaring My promises to you. You shall walk in victory for I am by your side. Hold tight to the freedom you have gained thus far, don't give up any ground to your enemy. You lose ground and victory when you agree with him. Fill yourself with pure things, good things, like My Word. If you fall, I will be there, lifting you up without condemnation.

Be easy on yourself, for I am patient and merciful. The great I AM is not a taskmaster but the lover of your soul. Remember to ask for My wisdom and strategies in defeating the devil in your life and others' lives. The strategy may be as simple as forgiveness and repentance, and other times you will need revelation and more detailed strategies. Ask and I will give you the tools and confidence to overcome.

Submit therefore to God. Resist the devil and he will flee from you.
James 4:7

Declaration

Christ has made me victorious over the devil.

Prayer

Abba Father, thank you for Your marvelous plans that defeated satan at the cross. I pray this reality of satan's defeat becomes a greater reality in the lives of all Your children. Holy Spirit, increase my wisdom and discernment in knowing where my enemy is hiding so I can pray effectively. Forgive me if I have agreed with what the enemy has been doing and saying. I declare that I will look above the circumstances surrounding me to find Christ in them. Increase my sensitivity to the Holy Spirit in order that I may stand strong in my authority and declare to the enemy, take a hike. In Christ our Lord. Amen.

His Heart for Me

Are you doing battle with the enemy? Are you tired from rebuking him and still having the same issues? Have you asked God for specific strategies in removing the devil from your life? If you haven't, ask Him today and follow through with what He reveals. Ask the Lord to disclose where you have agreed with the enemy in your life and in the lives of your family.

Day 47

Called and Qualified

And we know that God causes all things to work together for good to those who love God, to those who are called according to His purpose.
Romans 8:28

Thought for the Day: Your weaknesses provide an opportunity for God's strength to shine in your life.

"God doesn't call the equipped, He equips the called." The Bible teaches us that God chose imperfect people. They had strengths and weaknesses, just like we do. David was known as a man after God's own heart, but he also committed adultery with Bathsheba, and had Uriah, her husband, killed.

God called Moses to lead the children of Israel out of Egypt, but Moses felt inadequate for the task. Moses used his lack of eloquent speech as an excuse to disobey God. Doubting God's ability caused Moses to plead with the Lord to send the message through someone else. The Lord actually got quite angry with Moses for his unbelief. Moses got in the way of what God wanted to do. What did our patient God do for Moses? He found a replacement. Aaron spoke for Moses. This was not God's plan, but the future of a nation was at stake, so He found someone to help Moses.

Feeling the weight of the call and looking at our lack of qualifications may cause us to say no or doubt God's ability to work through us. I have a habit of dragging my feet, but I still go, asking God to increase my faith as I do His will. Even if I look like a fool to others, I will not refuse the Lord's request to do uncomfortable things. My heart's desire is that God would be greatly glorified through my obedience.

The Lord's Heart

Child, don't doubt My ability to use you, like Moses did, for I know you. I ordained your days before you were born. There is a book in heaven inscribed by Me concerning your life, it is forever before Me. I ordered your parents' thoughts when it came time to pick your name. From day one, I have watched you. I know how many hairs are on your head, every detail about you, and what you are called to do. There are godly passions and desires in your heart that I placed there, and I will fan the flame so they burn more brightly. Doors of opportunity are opening around you. I will highlight the path you are to take. You can do what I have called you to do.

Take your eyes off your strengths thinking that by them you shall fulfill your calling. You can only fulfill your calling by trusting in My ability to equip you for the task. I like it when you know your weaknesses to the point of knowing this: I can't do it, but God can do it through me. You don't have to be a trained speaker to have Me use you to speak. Your promotion will not be because of your intelligence or abilities. You are promoted because of your proven character and pure heart. I look at your heart, your submission, and honesty.

Moses looked at his abilities when I asked him to be My mouthpiece. This frustrated Me, but I answered his request and allowed Aaron to speak for him. Moses eventually trusted in My ability to use him to speak and he became the great leader I called him to be.

How about you? Will you trust Me to make you all I want you to be? It's up to you. Trust in Me, My child, for I love you.

And looking at them Jesus said to them,
"With people this is impossible, but with God all things are possible."
Matthew 19:26

Declaration

I will accept my assignments from God.

Prayer

Abba Father, thank you for equipping me with every good thing to do Your will, working in me that which is pleasing in Your sight, through Jesus Christ, to whom be the glory forever and ever. I will walk by the spirit of wisdom in my callings. I will have unshakable faith in what You can do through me. I will not ask You to get another to fulfill my calling. Holy Spirit, thank you for making me flexible and obedient to my Maker. I give You full permission to get my attention when I am not walking in His ways. In Christ our Lord. Amen.

His Heart for Me

What has the Lord called you to do? Don't firmly plant your feet on one calling but be flexible to go His way. Ask the Lord if you have refused Him in any way. If He reveals an area, be determined to obey Him. Repent for any unbelief you have in what God can do through you. Write out your strengths and weaknesses. God likes to call us to operate out of our weaknesses. If you have thoughts like, "I can't do this," it might just be the thing He calls you to do someday.

Day 48

Stretchy Wineskins

No one puts new wine into old wineskins; otherwise the wine will burst the skins, and the wine is lost and the skins as well; but one puts new wine into fresh wineskins.
Mark 2:22

Thought for the Day: My wineskin will remain fresh and new as I allow the Lord to mold and stretch me with His sanctifying work.

In the days of old, people would use a goatskin to carry their water or wine. The skins were cleaned well and sewn on the sides making them water tight. As new wine was put into these skins, they would stretch and become thinner from the fermentation process. Putting new wine into an old wineskin would be asking for trouble. Once the new wine began to ferment, the bag would burst.

When Jesus gave this parable, He was addressing the Pharisees. The religious leaders were angry with Jesus because He wasn't obeying all of their rules and also dined with sinners. Jesus came and turned their world upside down and inside out. He allowed His disciples to pick grain on the Sabbath and they didn't fast. (Mark 2:18-20,23-28) Jesus even let the adulteress woman go free. Jesus was inviting them to embrace the new wineskin of grace and love, but the Pharisees wanted to stick with the old and worn-out wineskin of self-righteousness and legalism.

We are still guilty of this today. It's more appealing to add Jesus to our old wineskin, our old way of doing things, and keep our old nature. We need to allow Jesus to turn our world upside down and inside out as well.

Several years ago, I was at a women's retreat struggling with what the Lord wanted to do in my life. I was struggling because I was comfortable with the "old way."

A woman approached me and asked if she could pray over me. I agreed even though I didn't know her. She started praying in tongues over me. (It was the first time I had experienced this.) The interpretation of those tongues came a few seconds later: "You can't put new wine into old wineskins. Get rid of the old so you can embrace the new." This hit me like a ton of bricks. The Lord was asking me to give up my old ways so He could do something new in me. This is His desire for you today. Throw out the old and embrace the new thing that Jesus wants to do in and through you.

The Lord's Heart

Let Me stretch your wineskin. You can't put new wine in old wineskins or they will burst. There are some mindsets, habits, and patterns in your life that need to be re-written. Make room for the new that I want to do in you. The old ways of doing things don't mix well with the new ways. I will fill you with the purest of wines from heaven and you shall drink and pour out freely. Cultivate and stir up the gifts within you. Be willing to allow Me to stretch and transform you, as I expand your vision of who you are and who I am to you. Don't be content with your current spiritual state. If I reveal something in your life that is not pleasing to Me, let go of it, for I have something better for you. My gift to you is a new wineskin that will always be flexible and stretchy; one that will not get old and burst. I am calling you to embrace the new. Though it may be uncomfortable at first, persevere, great will be your reward.

And He was also telling them a parable: "No one tears a piece of cloth from a new garment and puts it on an old garment; otherwise he will both tear the new, and the piece from the new will not match the old."

Luke 5:36

Declaration

I will allow the Lord to stretch and transform me continually.

Prayer

Abba Father, I surrender my will for Yours. I want to remain flexible and moldable. Move me out of my complacency to a life filled with great zeal for You and Your ways. Holy Spirit, encourage me to not be afraid of the new and unknown things coming my way. As I embrace the new, fill me with a spirit of joy and excitement. I will accept the new wine You want to pour into me. Today I declare that my new wine will have an enormous effect on Your Kingdom. My wineskins shall be large and overflowing with Your love and goodness. In Christ of Lord. Amen.

His Heart for Me

Do you need a new wineskin? Have you become hard or brittle so you are unable to be stretched or receive something new from the Lord? Have you gotten comfortable and complacent with where you are in life? Are your heart and soul craving more of God? Spend some time with the Lord concerning your answers to these questions. I encourage you to listen to the song, *New Wine* by Hillsong.

Day 49

The Promise of Eternal Rewards

I press on toward the goal for the prize of
the upward call of God in Christ Jesus.
Philippians 3:14

Thought for the Day: I am an overcomer.

What can we do to overcome the trials, storms, and unpleasant circumstances in our lives? Stop asking God to remove them and start looking for God in the storm. Stand on the truth and declare God's promises over our situations until we see a breakthrough, a miracle, answered prayer. Pray constantly, trusting in God's good plans for us, even if we don't understand what He is doing and why we are going through so much pain. Choose to praise Him in the middle of the storm. Be grateful for every blessing God has given you, big or small. This won't be easy! Our flesh will complain and grumble but press on, Christian soldier, for your reward in heaven is great.

To persevere to the end, we must set our eyes on the goal, not our trials. If we focus on the storm, we may become discouraged and lose hope. As humans, we are often motivated by the reward. God knows that, so in the scriptures, He outlines our eternal rewards.

In Revelation 2-3, John is shown a vision by the Lord and instructed to write letters to the seven churches that were in Asia. These letters were full of encouragement regarding the things they were doing right, areas where they needed to improve, and the promise of the reward that awaited them because of their faithfulness. These are the rewards Christ promises those who persevere to the end. (Personalize these promises by inserting your name where it says "you, he or him.")

1. To him who overcomes, I will grant to eat of the tree of life which is in the Paradise of God. (Revelation 2:7)

2. I will give you the crown of life and you will not be hurt by the second death. (Revelation 2:10-11)

3. I will give some of the hidden manna, and I will give him a white stone, and a new name written on the stone. (Revelation 2:17)

4. I WILL GIVE AUTHORITY OVER THE NATIONS and I will give him the morning star. (Revelation 2:26-28)

5. He will thus be clothed in white garments and I will not erase his name from the book of life, and I will confess his name before My Father and before His angels. (Revelation 3:5-6)

6. I will make him a pillar in the temple of My God, I will write on him the name of My God, and the name of the city of My God, the new Jerusalem. (Revelation 3:12-13)

7. I will grant him to sit down with Me on My throne. (Revelation 3:21-22)

As you can see, our perseverance through suffering and godly living has great rewards. Be encouraged today that we are overcomers through Christ, our Lord. Even on your darkest days, know that God is for you and not against you. We are more than conquerors through Him who loved us so. Great will be your reward in heaven.

The Lord's Heart

I have made you to be an overcomer. You are no longer a slave to fear or past addictions. Set your mind on the things above, dear child, and not the circumstances surrounding you. Have a heart of praise like Paul and Silas, when they were chained together in a dark and dreary prison. For in the midst of their pain and suffering they still praised Me for who I am, and this brought others to salvation in Christ. Your suffering will also bring others to Christ. Choose your actions wisely for others are watching how you respond.

Your praise through pain brings Me glory. Paul and Silas didn't cry out to be delivered or cast demons out of the guards. Instead they praised Me and set their hearts and minds on My Kingdom and I delivered them. Don't trust your feelings, trust Me during times of suffering, and I will deliver you.

You will learn to overcome all the temptations and trials in your life. Learning to overcome is a process of walking through the storm: hurricane, tornado, or tsunami. Your faithfulness in trials and temptations shapes you into a pillar that is unmovable. As you overcome the battles in your life, first one, then another, you will stand in My strength, radiant from My glory in you. When I hand you the stone with your new name on it, you will be able to identify yourself with this new name for it will represent what you have overcome in your life. I long to place the crown of life on your head and My Son longs to confess your name before Me. The great I AM is faithful to help you overcome! Ask for My help.

Behold, I am coming quickly, and My reward is with Me,
to render to every man according to what he has done.
Revelation 22:12

Declaration

My suffering has purpose.

Prayer

Abba Father, it is hard to understand with my mind that You are good while ordaining some of my trials and sufferings. Let my spirit and heart understand Your goodness while my mind takes a back seat to trying to figure everything out. I declare that I will exercise my faith in trusting You and Your plans. I will remember that You are a good Father. I will remember that everything I endure or suffer while on earth will be turned for my good. I declare that my enemy does not have the final word on my circumstances. Holy Spirit, empower me with strength to endure it all.

In Christ our Lord. Amen.

His Heart for Me

How do you view your suffering? Ask the Holy Spirit to show you the good in your trials and sufferings and write it down. Has salvation been brought to another through your actions during suffering? Has someone been brought closer to the Lord because you trusted Him when it looked like He turned His back on you? What has God helped you to overcome? Share it with someone. It could be the very thing they need to hear to help them overcome their battle.

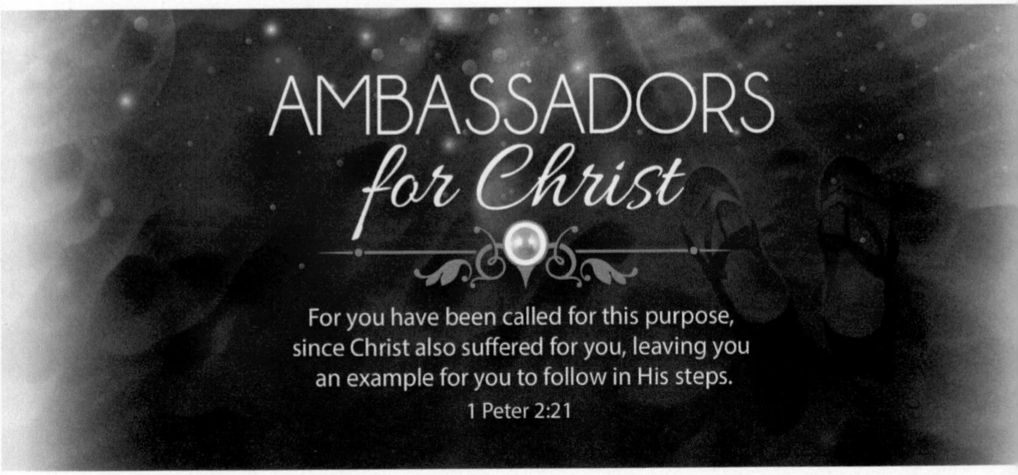
AMBASSADORS
for Christ
For you have been called for this purpose,
since Christ also suffered for you, leaving you
an example for you to follow in His steps.
1 Peter 2:21

Finding Our Identity in Christ

Just as He chose us in Him before the foundation of the world, that we would be holy and blameless before Him. In love He predestined us to adoption as sons through Jesus Christ to Himself, according to the kind intention of His will, to the praise of the glory of His grace, which He freely bestowed on us in the Beloved.

Ephesians 1:4-6

Thought for the Day: I am a royal priest; an ambassador of Christ.

Finding my true identity in Christ has been a long struggle. I was wrapped in a web of lies being fed to me by my enemy. Since birth, the devil has been attempting to steal my life and my true identity. Although, I can't blame it all on the enemy. I chose to believe those lies. For many years, I rejected Christ's sacrifice of love for me.

Many of the lies kept me from pursuing the life God had for me. I believed I was stupid and would never amount to anything. Why should I try? One person can't change the world. I am fatherless. I believed that if I died no one would care. I was "just" a mom, a housewife.

Believing that I was stupid kept me from going to college. Once this lie was exposed, I went to bible college, did very well, and graduated. Believing that I was fatherless was the most devastating because I wandered around like an orphan, struggling, lonely, and lost without a place of acceptance. Even though I have no earthly father figure in my life, I have a heavenly Father who adores me and is always there for me. He is the best daddy anyone could hope for.

Yes, I am a housewife and mom but the devil twisted them to make them sound unimportant. Shame and guilt for not contributing financially to our household kept me from seeing the value in being a homeschooling mother and wife.

I needed to belong somewhere, so my identity hung on the titles I acquired as I increased my expertise in an area. By the grace of God, He allowed me to get so frustrated jumping from one identity to another that I finally abandoned my fruitless efforts and found my true identity in Him.

As we search for our purpose, we often look to the things of this world - our job or social status. Were you really born just to get married, have kids, and work for the rest of your life? Thank the Lord there is much more to life than that. What we do for a living is only a temporary source of money. We may enjoy our job, but it is only what we do, it doesn't define who we are. All of us are called to be ministers for Christ, not only those with a pastor's title. It's important that we don't put our pastors on a high pedestal, because they are humans, just like you and me. Being a pastor is where God has called them to serve Him. Where has God placed you?

Early in my journey one of the tools that God used to guide me to the truth about who I was in Him was an excerpt from Dr. Neil Anderson's book, *Living Free in Christ* called "Who Am I?" There was a list of scriptures declaring who I was in Christ. As I repeated them several times a day, they became rooted in my heart. My mind was renewed to think like Jesus as I quoted these over myself. I finally started to believe my true identity in Christ. We need to proclaim God's truth of who we are daily instead of what our enemy and others say about us.

The Lord's Heart

You are My child. I have adopted you into My Kingdom. You may be without an earthly father, but I have always been your Father from day one. So, the truth is this: you are not fatherless. I predestined you for adoption long ago. You are My special treasure. I shall bring you to the fullness of all truth concerning your true identity. You are one with Me in spirit. You are no longer a slave but My son or daughter, heirs in My Kingdom. I created you in My image. So, love yourself. When you love yourself in a healthy way, you are loving Me. Since the day of your baptism you have been clothed with Christ. You are seated with Us in the heavenlies. Oh, how I long to be with all My children in paradise. There shall be a joyous celebration in My Kingdom when all the saints are present.

Do you want to know your true identity? Look at Christ. You mirror Him. Don't put your identity in your job or even the things I have called you to do, but in the fact that you are My beloved child. My heart hurts to see you miss out on knowing your true identity and what belongs to you. Your true identity in Christ will be attacked, so arm yourself with the scriptures that speak truth about who you are. Do you remember that satan hit Jesus with this identity question: "If you are the Son of God, tell these stones to become bread." My Son's identity was attacked first and so will yours be. Know who you are! The enemy knows that if he can get you to question your identity or confuse you about who you are, you will not reach your full potential. He is scared of you. For he knows that I have mighty works for you to accomplish for My Kingdom, but you must know your identity to accomplish them all. Do you know what is available to you as a child of God? Everything that was available to Christ is yours.

No longer do I call you slaves, for the slave does not know what his master is doing; but I have called you friends, for all things that I have heard from My Father I have made known to you. You did not choose Me but I choose you, and appointed you that you would go and bear fruit, and that your fruit would remain, so that whatever you ask of the Father in My name He may give to you.
John 15:15

Declaration

I am a saint and friend of Jesus.

Prayer

Abba Father, oh how I thank you, Lord, for adopting me into Your Kingdom. I am seated with You in the heavenly places right now. Thank you for preparing a room for me in heaven and caring so much for me. What an honor it is to be considered a saint at salvation. Your ways are so great! I declare that I am a joint heir with Christ and will be welcomed to feast with Him at the greatest wedding feast of all time. Holy Spirit, open our hearts to receive more revelation about who we are in Christ. I command all veils or blinders placed on my identity to be removed right now! In Jesus mighty and powerful name! In Christ our Lord. Amen.

His Heart for Me

Who do you say you are? With whom do you agree concerning yourself? I encourage you to write down all the "who am I" proclamations and put them on your refrigerator. I look at mine every day and declare a couple each day. Ask the Lord if you have accepted any false identities about yourself and seek to find the truth concerning that lie. Ask the Spirit of truth to help you.

Day 51

Salt and Light

You are the salt of the earth; but if the salt has become tasteless, how can it be made salty again? It is no longer good for anything, except to be thrown out and trampled under foot by men. You are the light of the world. A city set on a hill cannot be hidden; nor does anyone light a lamp and put it under a basket, but on the lampstand, and it gives light to all who are in the house. Let your light shine before men in such a way that they may see your good works, and glorify your Father who is in heaven.

Matthew 5:13-16

Thought for the Day: God has made me salty and bright; a preservative and light to others.

Jesus said we would be salt to the earth. In the Hebrew Bible, salt is both a disinfectant and a preservative. To me, the salt represents our flavor, our peace, and joy. When you add salt to water, the salt quickly becomes diluted. Christians can become diluted and lose our flavor, peace, and joy when we encounter fiery trials and unpleasant experiences.

How are we to remain salty to the world and those around us? By reading the Bible and staying connected to God. We get to choose how we will respond to the circumstances in our life. One choice will keep us salty and the other will make us good for nothing. When we hold on to bitterness, anger, or a victim mentality, we've lost our saltiness.

How can we get it back? Forgive and repent, and your flavor will return to you. Then you will bring that sweet flavor of Jesus back to yourself and to others.

Followers of Christ give light to others by doing what He did, our light dispels the darkness. The more time we spend with Jesus, the brighter we become.

When my husband and I started going out on the streets to minister, I had a really hard time being salt and light to others. I wanted to run and hide. My face would get red and hot from embarrassment. Stumbling over my words as I prayed, my heart raced with fear from being around people that were different than me. Eventually I learned to remove the blanket covering my lamp by speaking salty words of truth to others and believing differently.

The Lord's Heart

Your red face, racing heart, and desire to run away are tactics the enemy uses against you which cause you to get distracted and flee from completing the assignments I have placed before you. The devil wants you to focus on your jumbled words and hot face, instead of Me. He doesn't want you to speak or shine brightly for Me, so he will do whatever it takes to cause you to withdraw. Satan takes great pleasure in stirring up anxiety, fear, and doubt in My children, in hopes of keeping them from fulfilling their assignments. The devil is a master at speaking lies to your mind and body. Be alert to your enemy's ways, and don't accept his lies as your own truth. Only My words and My promises are true. When you stop being embarrassed by renewing your mind with My truth and putting your faith in Me, satan will lose interest and slink away.

Here is the truth.

You are My sunshine on earth, precious one. You are brighter than you realize. You are the salt that brings taste and life to others. The light in your eyes attracts others. They see Me in you, that is why they are drawn to you. They see My purity through you. A simple smile can penetrate the hardest of hearts. When they see you suffer, and still trust and hope in Me, it breaks down walls of protection. When you are transparent and honest, it frees others to do the same. Don't pretend all is well, if it is not.

The great I AM is directing your steps and aligning you to His will. I will never harm you. I am your perfect Father who loves you perfectly. I still love you when you do the things you wish you didn't. You are always welcome to come to Me. You don't have to be perfect before I will accept you and communicate with you. Just come! Don't meditate on your sins or mistakes, simply repent and come unhindered to Me.

My arms are wide open ready to receive you. Truly, truly, I say to you, My Son's blood covers all your sins. The enemy would like to beat you up and make you feel like you can't approach Me. Don't listen! Turn a deaf ear to him.

My child, your obedience is pleasing to Me. My Spirit will guide you into all truth and empower you to do My will. I will be there holding your hand every step of the way. Call out to Me, for I will help you. Don't lean on your own understanding but Mine and Mine alone. My Spirit will help you.

Arise, shine; for your light has come,
And the glory of the Lord has risen upon you.
Isaiah 60:1

Declaration

I will maintain my saltiness by dwelling in His presence.

Prayer

Abba Father, thank you for making me a light to those who are in darkness, those who are perishing. I will keep my light shining brightly by pursuing intimacy with Christ and Your words to me in scripture. I will meditate on Your love and promises to me, which will make my words salty and delicious to others. Holy Spirit, help me to focus my attention on You and what You are doing instead of what the enemy is trying to do in my mind or body. Clothe me continually with peace and joy.

In Christ our Lord. Amen.

His Heart for Me

Where do you shine brightly for the Lord? Do you see good fruit in your relationships? Are there any areas in your life that need more light or salt? Are there any sins or mistakes you haven't forgiven yourself for yet? Invite the Holy Spirit to talk to you today about your lamp and your saltiness. Record what He says here.

Day 52

Peacemakers vs. Peacekeepers

If possible, so far as it depends on you, be at peace with all men.
Romans 12:18

Thought for the Day: I carry the peace of Christ within me. Sometimes that peace will bring peace to others, and other times, it will bring conviction and conflict.

God has called us to be peacemakers, people who make peace everywhere we go. However, if we are speaking truth like Jesus did, others might get offended. We can't be afraid to speak what is right and true to others. When we don't speak truth in order to keep the peace, we are peacekeepers (people pleasers) rather than peacemakers (truth speakers).

Courage is the trait of a "peacemaker" because they face conflict head on. Peacemakers bring joy, happiness, and peace into a room as well as conviction, and sometimes conflict, with those who are doing wrong. Peacemakers will speak the hard truth because they love others and want the best for them. Peacemakers won't feel threatened when others have different opinions. They are open to looking at both sides of an argument and willing to meet somewhere in the middle, even if that means agreeing to disagree. If there are disagreements, they will seek reconciliation. (Matthew 5:23-24) Secure in their own identity and convictions, peacemakers will not let others manipulate them. They will stand strong on the truth.

Timidity is the trait of a "peacekeeper" because they avoid conflict at all costs. Peacekeepers are people who allow others to manipulate them into believing that the peacekeeper's opinions and convictions are not important. They are typically quiet and shy people that keep the truth to themselves. Peacekeepers will agree verbally with others, while internally disagreeing. This might sound like the nice thing to do but it is dishonest and can have devastating effects on the peacekeeper. Those who try to keep the peace will work hard at pretending nothing is wrong. They appear more spiritually mature by keeping quiet and demonstrating their ability to endure hard things.

Peacekeeping is a habit that must be demolished for it serves no one well. Maturity comes by working through the conflicts and offenses. We may need to be offended so we can repent and draw closer to God. Jesus loved the religious leaders enough to speak the truth. He wanted them to be drawn into a real loving relationship with the Father. True love is loving others enough to speak the hard truth from a place of humility, gentleness, and patience making every effort to restore the relationship. May we all seek to follow the example of Jesus and be peacemakers in the world today.

The Lord's Heart

Beloved, I have made you to be a peacemaker, not a peacekeeper. Peacemakers operate in My authority and wisdom. They have high hopes and walk in humility. Peacemakers do not ignore conflict. They wade through conflict with the help of My Spirit. Peacemakers understand that repentance is necessary for true peace to be created.

Peacekeepers sacrifice righteousness for the sake of peace. Peacekeepers walk like they are walking on eggshells being ever so careful to not offend or say anything wrong. Peacemakers take aim at the heart of the problem, the heart of people, including themselves, and ask Me for wisdom. It is healthy to discuss differences in opinions, emotions, fears, misunderstandings, and offenses. All of these things should be brought into the light, so they can be dealt with instead of letting them simmer under the surface and turn into unforgiveness and bitterness. Go to great lengths to make peace as long as it depends on you. However, remember that you cannot make someone else be at peace. You can't make others treat you right and kind. If their actions rise to the level of abuse, you need to remove yourself. They are responsible for their actions. Your responsibility is to forgive and make peace, if possible. My world needs more peacemakers, choose to follow Me.

Blessed are the peacemakers, for they shall be called sons of God.
Matthew 5:9

Declaration

Christ didn't avoid conflict to keep peace and neither will I.

Prayer

Abba Father, protect those who are in abusive relationships and provide a way of escape. Empower me to be a peacemaker every place I go. I declare I will not cower and feel intimidated by those who have angry outbursts or temper tantrums because of the truth I speak. Holy Spirit, enable me to love others beyond measure, as I wade through conflicts or disagreements. I will be brave enough to seek reconciliation and not sweep my offenses under a rug in hopes of them going away. Lord, I do not seek to offend but seek to draw others closer to You through repentance and forgiveness just as I draw close to You in the same fashion. In Christ our Lord. Amen.

His Heart for Me

Do your actions match the one who is a peacemaker or peacekeeper? Are you offended? Is the offense a true offense or a perceived offense due to assumption or suspicion? Seek the Lord and His answers concerning every offense and disagreement. We humans have a habit of making things seem worse than they really are. How can you start being more like the peacemaker? Ask Christ and record His ideas here.

If you are being physically abused, please seek help. Talk to your pastor or someone you trust. If you live in the United States and need help contact: Focus on the Family helpline 1-800-232-6459.

Day 53

Our Youth, Our Future

But the Lord said to me, "Do not say, 'I am a youth,'
Because everywhere I send you, you shall go,
And all that I command you, you shall speak."
Jeremiah 1:7

Thought for the Day: Christians who invest in youth today, create leaders for tomorrow.

God left us in charge of educating the young, both our biological and spiritual children, in the way they should go. Our youth need mature Christians to pour truth, light, and love into their lives. They need someone who will share their life struggles, thoughts, feelings, and questions. Without this safety net, we see the resulting tragedies daily reported in the newspaper headlines.

Our youth need our experience and insight because of the trials and testings we have encountered. Much of the rebellion we see coming from our youth is the result of mature Christians not fulfilling their duty to teach them to live self-controlled lives – upright and godly lives. They need spiritual fathers and mothers teaching them to live for God and not themselves. We are not perfect and will make mistakes but that can't stop us from trying to guide the youth that God entrusts in our care.

The best mentors point us to the highest mentor, Christ, our Lord. They point us to obey all Christ's instructions. As mentors, we must teach our mentees to rely, not on us as their spiritual parent, but on their heavenly Father. We must seek a balanced relationship with them and keep Christ as the wisest and greatest counselor.

Many of the most influential leaders in the Old and New Testament were young men. Jeremiah was only seventeen years old when God called him to minister to the people of Judah. Jeremiah doubted his qualifications because he was so young. (Jeremiah 1:6-7) How many of our youth today think the same way? Samuel was around twelve or thirteen when God called him to the ministry. And with Eli's guidance, Samuel responded, "Speak, Lord, for your servant is listening." How about David? David was just a young man when he defeated Goliath, the giant, who was terrorizing the Israelites. And Samuel anointed David, in his youth, with God's promise that one day he would reign as the King of Israel.

God calls many in their younger years. It is important for all of us to sow good seed into our youth and pray for the next generation that God is raising up to accomplish His purposes.

The Lord's Heart

I am calling the youth of today to action! Throughout history, I have called young ones into My service, but there will be an increase in the young doing My will. They will have such a burning desire to obey Me that nothing shall stop them. My mighty strong anointing on them will break through strongholds. Your mighty and awesome God is sending the Holy Spirit on willing children who will bring My purifying fire around the world. Their zeal for Me will cause the darkness to flee in their presence. The darkness won't be able to withstand the purity within them. Oh, the purity of My children who will speak on My behalf shall crush the shackles off those lost in darkness.

This outpouring on our youth will stir up the older generation to action and love. Older women are being called to teach the younger women. Older men to teach the younger men. Teach them the ways of godliness, to walk in great power. Some will think these youth are being rebellious and crazy and accuse them of seeking signs from heaven instead of Me. But the truth is, the great I AM is calling them to action. Those who truly walk in relationship with Me will light up the whole room and My presence will manifest. Don't reject this move of My Spirit upon the youth. They hunger to obey Me in everything. Invest your time and energy in those who are younger in your homes, churches, and your workplace.

It will come about after this That I will pour out My Spirit on all mankind; And your sons and daughter will prophesy, Your old men will dream dreams, Your young men will see visions.
Joel 2:28

Declaration

I will seek to pour heart knowledge into the young around me. I will seek to direct them in the ways of the Lord.

Prayer

Abba Father, You are so glorious. Thank you for giving me the responsibility to teach the younger women and men around me. Holy Spirit, empower me to walk an upright and godly life so I can teach others well. Encourage me to invest my time and energy in the young. Lord, I ask that You perfect me in Your love for others and give me an enormous amount of patience to fulfill this great privilege of discipling others. Bring a healthy balance to all mentor/mentee relationships where You are the wisest and highest counselor. May all Your children seek to be more intimate with You, Papa. In Christ our Lord. Amen.

His Heart for Me

Do you take time to listen and instruct the young among you? It is our responsibility to lead the young around us in the way they should go, the ways of the Lord. You have the experience and answers someone else needs. Ask God who He wants you to pour into and record it below. Then be faithful in sharing what you have learned along the way with them.

Day 54

The Faithful Watchmen

On your walls, O Jerusalem, I have appointed watchmen;
All day and all night they will never keep silent.
You who remind the Lord, take no rest for yourselves.
Isaiah 62:6

Thought for the Day: I will keep watch for what He will say to me and take action in prayer and deeds accordingly.

In ancient times, watchmen (typically prophets) stood guard either on a tower or on the city's walls, to warn the people of coming trouble. The typical watching hours were from 6 p.m. to 6 a.m. When the watchman saw trouble coming, he would sound an alarm by blowing a shofar, which could be heard at great distances. The watchman's job was to be taken seriously by staying awake, protecting the citizens, and giving warnings when needed. In Isaiah 52:7-10, we also see the watchmen shouting for joy as the Lord stretches out His hand to restore.

Jesus commands His disciples to watch and pray several times in the gospels. The word "watch" in Greek is "Gregopeo." It has the sense of being "vigilant", "to keep awake", "to be on the alert", and "to keep one's eyes open." Do you remember what the disciples did on the night of Jesus' arrest? They fell asleep while He prayed and sweat blood from His anguish. Jesus wanted His friends to intercede and watch for Him.

God has called many in the Body of Christ to be watchmen. Men and women alike are still needed to keep watch in our homes, churches, schools, in every place we step. These are people who are courageous enough to sound the alarm by opening their mouths to give those warnings when needed. Watchmen of today are filled with the power of Holy Spirit to be highly accurate intercessors which happens as they spend time with Jesus, cultivating a deep relationship with Him.

It is important to pray in the night hours because our enemy is wide awake, scheming for the day, setting up our demise while we are sleeping. We are protected from the devil and need not fear him. However, I have been convicted to pray once a week during the second or third watch hours, believing that our nightly prayers set the course and override the enemy's plans for our day and the day of others.

I believe every child of God has been given a specific time of day to watch, pray, and discern what God is doing and destroy the works of the enemy in our midst through prayer and revelation from the Father. Whether that is an hour during one of the eight watches of the day or a full three-hour watch, the Lord will reveal to you, your responsibility as a watchman or watchwoman.

The Eight Prayer Watches

First Watch: (Evening Watch) 6:00 P.M. – 9:00 P.M.

Matthew 14:15-23 Jesus feeds five thousand and then goes to pray.
Mark 1:32 Jesus healed at this hour.

Second Watch: 9:00 P.M—12:00 A.M.

Psalm 119:62 At midnight I shall rise and give thanks to you.
Luke 12:35-40 We are commanded to be awake, while we wait for our master's return, and open the door when He knocks.

Third Watch: (Breaking of Day Watch) 12:00 A.M.—3:00 A.M.

Acts 16:25-34 Paul and Silas were released from prison during this watch. A jailer was baptized, saved, washed wounds, and fed others.
Judges 16:3-4 Samson escaped from Gaza at midnight.

Fourth Watch: (Morning Watch) 3:00 A.M.—6:00 A.M.

Matthew 14:25 Jesus comes walking on water during the fourth watch.

Fifth Watch: 6:00 A.M.—9:00 A.M.

Acts 2:15 The Holy Spirit descended on the day of Pentecost during this watch.

Sixth Watch: 9:00 A.M.—12:00 P.M.

Mark 15:25 It was the third hour (9 a.m.) when they crucified Christ and then darkness came upon the face of the earth around 12 p.m.

Seventh Watch: 12:00 P.M.—3:00 P.M.

Matthew 27:45-50 Complete darkness saturated the earth during this entire watch. Our Lord died at the end of the seventh watch, the ninth hour.

Eighth Watch: 3:00 P.M.—6:00 P.M.

Matthew 27:50-54 The veil from the temple was torn during these hours, rocks split, tombs were opened, and many realized they had put to death the Son of God.

The Lord's Heart

Arise from your slumber and be alert, beloved. All My children are called to watch and pray for themselves and others. My children are mighty intercessors full of discernment and power from on high. My watchmen have eyes like an eagle. The great I AM is giving you extraordinarily strong vision so you can sound the alarm way in advance and give those who are complacent and far from Me time to wake up. Blessed is he/she who resists temptation and crucifies the flesh. I am giving my watchmen and women strength in their flesh to stay wake. Persevere in watching and listening to what I will say to you and pray through it, asking Me for greater understanding and wisdom. The great and mighty I AM is making your flesh strong so you won't suffer any ill effects from losing sleep. However, be wise, beloved. You do need to rest and take care of yourself.

My watchmen have the tools to set the captives free. They have the mantle of praise and wear a garland of strength. The oil of gladness will continually be upon them as a safeguard keeping them from discouragement. Hopelessness and discouragement from seeing evil rise will be extinguished by the oil of gladness from heaven. Their trust in Me shall soar and be unshakable.

The great I AM is sending His Son at an hour you do not know. He shall descend upon the earth with a shout, with the voice of the archangel and shofar. Be ready, My child, stay alert! Blessed is the one whom I find alert and waiting for My Son's return.

What I say to you I say to all, "Be on the alert."
Mark 13:37

Declaration

I will stand on my guard post; watching and praying
according to what He speaks to me.

Prayer

Abba Father, thank you for giving me greater vision. Thank you for the oil of gladness that keeps me encouraged while I intercede. Holy Spirit, thank you for a lifelong supply of strength and wisdom from above. Keep me alert. I ask that the scripture verse, "pray without ceasing" becomes a reality and a heightened responsibility for every Child of God this year. Remove the blanket off Your watchmen and women. Raise them up in our churches, homes, and schools. In every place where evil is rising, put a watchman and strengthen them to the utmost. Fill them with Your words and give them the unction to open wide their mouths to speak those warnings in love. In Christ our Lord. Amen.

His Heart for Me

God has commanded you to be watchful and pray. Do you unknowingly find yourself praying at the same time every day? Have you considered that to be your "watch"—your time to pray? Do you wake at 3 a.m. not knowing why? Ask the Lord what watch specifically you have been assigned, how often, and for how long, and record it here.

Day 55

Your Commission as a Christ Follower

And Jesus came up and spoke to them, saying, "All authority has been given to Me in heaven and on earth. "Go therefore and make disciples of all the nations, baptizing them in the name of the Father and the Son and the Holy Spirit, teaching them to observe all that I commanded you; and lo, I am with you always, even to the end of the age."
Matthew 28:18-20

Thought for the Day: I have been custom-built for making other disciples.

When I became a follower of Christ, I didn't have a clue what it meant to be a Christian. I just wanted to be saved from hell.

After attending church every Sunday for about six months, I remember thinking, "Is this what it means to be a Christian?" It seemed so pointless and boring. There has got to be more to the Christian walk was a constant echo in my heart. Receiving my "spiritual food" on Sunday wasn't enough to sustain me through the week. When I took the time to read the Word of God, I didn't understand what I was reading, so I stopped reading it. Unfortunately, I didn't understand the importance of reading the Word daily and asking God for wisdom while I read.

Ten years later, when I received the Holy Spirit and tongues, the Lord showed me just how much more there was to the Christian life. I began having visions of Christ and heaven. I was constantly overwhelmed by His love and the "more" He was revealing to me.

There was a new burning desire in my heart to preach the word and go many places. I have always been pretty shy and quiet, so great fear gripped my heart with the thought of preaching the gospel abroad with signs and wonders following.

Because of God's great love for me and His desire to see these plans fulfilled, He personally commissioned me to preach Christ crucified through four of His angels. It was an encounter I will never forget. God told me to not be afraid and commanded me to go. I answered, "Yes, I will go whenever and wherever you tell me to go." As I wait for the fulfillment of this vision, I am faithfully sharing Christ where I live and in cities closeby.

After Jesus' death and resurrection, He appeared to His disciples one final time and commanded them "to go and make disciples of all nations," what we know as the Great Commission. Jesus' mandate is the same for us today. Some will be sent out a greater distance than others, but each of us has a responsibility to share Jesus with our families, friends, neighbors, and coworkers. We are to teach others the way of Christ and share our testimony of what He has done for us. There is no greater joy than seeing someone who is lost and headed for hell saved, adopted, and welcomed into the kingdom of God. All of heaven rejoices over the "one" that is saved. Another great joy is seeing others get filled with the Holy Spirit and set on fire to do His will.

From the fruit of our obedience, a new generation of believers will be raised up to passionately share their testimony and make disciples. In our churches, we will grow in maturity, hear sound teaching, and learn to serve others. But the fulfillment of the "Great Commission" begins outside the walls of our church as we love others and introduce them to the path of life.

The Lord's Heart

I have called you to act while you are living on earth. I have not called you to be comfortable or complacent in the church but to live a life of action for My Kingdom. I have given you My authority and the power of the Holy Spirit to help you complete your assignments of baptizing, making disciples, teaching the full truth about Me, raising the dead, healing the sick, and casting out demons. Everything I did you can do, and if you are willing, you can do more than Me. Take your faith and put it into action. I have commissioned you to make disciples as you go. This was My final instruction, not only for the eleven, but for all of God's children. It was a command for all believers not just ones that feel called to it specifically. Be committed to Me and committed to continuing My work on earth. I am with the Father now and desire for you to continue My work. I fulfilled every part of My assignment the Father had for Me, however, I left you My authority and power to continue what I started. There are cities and nations that still need to know about Me. Be bold and share the good news of your salvation, the source of your joy with others. Don't hold out for missions far away, your mission starts with your neighbor. I have commissioned every Christian to step out in faith and share the good news. Obey this command and your spiritual life will be changed forever. The great I AM is faithful to supply all your needs as you obey this command to increase My Kingdom here on earth.

And He said to them, "Go into all the world and preach the gospel to all creation. He who has believed and has been baptized shall be saved; but he who has disbelieved shall be condemned. These signs will accompany those who have believed: in My name they will cast out demons, they will speak with new tongues; they will pick up serpents, and if they drink any deadly poison, it will not hurt them; they will lay hands on the sick, and they will recover."

Mark 16:15-18

Declaration

I will live a missionary life where I currently live; seeking to help others.

Prayer

Abba Father, thank you that the Christian life is so full of life, purpose, love, and joy. I ask for continued strength to be bold in sharing our testimonies and the good news with others where we live. Holy Spirit, empower us to make disciples who will in turn make more disciples. May the truth of who You are continually be with us. Make us effectual doers of Your Word with great communications skills so we can know how to respond to each one in front of us. Break our hearts for what breaks Yours. Flood us with Your great compassion for those around us. In Christ our Lord. Amen.

His Heart for Me

Are you currently living a missional life as you seek to help those around you? Seek the Lord's will, concerning this command for you specifically. Where has He placed you at this time in your life? That is your mission field right now. Who has He put on your heart to share your testimony? Who does He want you to help with your gifts and abilities? What small or large steps can you take? I encourage you to not delay.

Afterword

In the arms of the Father, far away from fear.
Contentment and assurance of His love
You shall find when you draw near.
Come boldly to the throne of grace above.

Behold, the eyes of the Father are upon you
With arms wide open, longing to embrace
And excited to shower you with His love and affection.

You are secure in the arms of the Father
For He is proud of you.

When the storms come crashing and the thief is at your back
All you need to do is run and climb up onto His lap.
You'll find peace and comfort in the arms of the Father.
You'll find your strength and armor
So, stay away from Him no longer.

This book, *My Beloved*, is the fulfillment of a prophecy. In 2017, at a barn worship meeting, Victoria Patterson prophesied that I would write a book. She proclaimed that I already had some of the material saved. This was true because I record what the Lord speaks to me and what I see Him doing in my life. Lacking the skills to be a writer, I didn't think much more about it.

In February 2018, we had a prophetic word pronounced over the church we attend. "Many more books are coming out of this house." Not only was this word for several people in our church, but it was for me, and I knew it. It was my personal call from the Lord. Because I put faith in the prophecies spoken over me, it was time to take action.

First, I prayed and asked God to open doors for His will to be done. Then I set time aside every day to write, to see what He would do. Step by step, God has equipped me and taught me how to write. Financially, He supplied the funds to cover the costs. Just like clay in the potter's hands, I have become an "author" through the guidance of the Holy Spirit and ministering angels sent from heaven. Writing this book has been an amazing opportunity to trust Him to do what I thought I could not do. Rest assured that if God has called you to perform a task, He will supply what is needed to complete it, all for His glory!

These 55 days with you have been enjoyable. There is so much more on my heart that I would love to share but I shall leave you with these final thoughts. Continue to cultivate greater intimacy with God by asking Him questions and waiting for His reply. Jesus walked this earth, just as you are now, be encouraged by His example. You will stumble and fall but by His grace, Abba Father will pick you up and urge you to keep going. And finally, let the Holy Spirit guide you, ask for wisdom and you will receive it. Then walk in all God has for you.

The Christian life is exciting, adventurous, fun, and challenging - all at the same time. May freedom abound in your life both in the natural realm and in His spiritual realm.

Blessings and love,

Pam

About the Author

PAM BACANI is a pursuer of God's heart and an emerging prophetic voice in our time. The mother of two teens, one of which she still home-schools full time, Pam is a country girl through and through right down to her favorite cowboy boots. Most days you will find Pam in the barn, in the woods, or harvesting her garden. Pam's dream is to preach the full gospel of Jesus Christ in the power of the Holy Spirit with signs and wonders following. She lives to see and set the captives free and looks forward to raising the dead one day.

Pam and her husband of 24 years are radical followers of Christ who have a hunger to do all that Jesus did and more. They lead a prophetic evangelism outreach team reaching out to others through the leading of the Holy Spirit speaking salvation, purpose, identity, and the plans of Abba Father to all they meet. Their heart's desire is to see all of God's children walking in resurrection power as they encourage others to pursue an intimate relationship with Jesus.

Pam is a Global University graduate and a blogger for awomansheart.net. Co-author of *Our Favorite Old Testament Stories* compiled by Tina Ware-Walters, her short story, "A Contemporary Ruth and Naomi Relationship" will be published later in 2019. Pam and her family reside in Eastern Washington.